The Glory Years of the Pennsylvania Turnpike

This nighttime photograph of Rays Hill Tunnel is one of a series of images created by photojournalist Arthur Rothstein in 1942 that would help to glorify the brand new Pennsylvania Turnpike. (Library of Congress.)

On the Front Cover: An unidentified man views with awe the soon-to-open Pennsylvania Turnpike from high atop Clear Ridge Cut. (Herbert Gehr, the Life Images Collection–Getty Images.)

On the Back Cover: A vehicle exits Laurel Hill Tunnel just days before the opening of the Pennsylvania Turnpike in a promotional photograph created by the Westinghouse Electric Company to promote their tunnel lighting equipment. (Westinghouse Electric Company.)

THE GLORY YEARS OF THE PENNSYLVANIA TURNPIKE

MITCHELL E. DAKELMAN AND NEAL A. SCHORR

ISBN 978-1-4671-2404-1

Published by Arcadia Publishing
Charleston, South Carolina

Printed in the United States of America

Library of Congress Control Number: 2016949793

For all general information, please contact Arcadia Publishing:
Telephone 843-853-2070
Fax 843-853-0044
E-mail sales@arcadiapublishing.com
For customer service and orders:
Toll-Free 1-888-313-2665

Visit us on the Internet at www.arcadiapublishing.com

Contents

ACKNOWLEDGMENTS

The authors would like to express their sincere thanks to the following individuals for their assistance with the creation of this book:

To our mutual friend, train collector, and retired PENNDOT District 11-0 assistant district engineer for design Thomas C. Fox. His comments regarding the Pennsylvania Turnpike were part of the inspiration to not only acknowledge the turnpike's fall from grace, but also to explain why it correctly came to be known as "The World's Greatest Highway."

To Neal Wood, retired chief bridge engineer of the Pennsylvania Turnpike Commission, for sharing his thoughts on the use of non-air-entrained concrete to build the bridges on the original section of the turnpike.

To Carl DeFebo and Christine Baker, both of the Communications and Public Relations Department of the Pennsylvania Turnpike Commission, for confirming dates and facts and providing contemporary images of the turnpike.

To North Huntington Township engineer Andrew W. Blenko and historian Vagel Keller, both members of the National Model Railroad Association, for their assistance in providing historical information regarding several of the images in this book.

To Nancy Summers for her assistance in providing historical information.

To Russ Love, whose photographic work on the South Penn right-of-way proved to be invaluable in the identification of the location of several South Penn tunnel images.

To Steven Schorr, who familiarized his father with several features of Google Maps, thereby making possible positive identification of the location of many images contained in this book.

And finally, to Caroline Schorr, for her patience with her father and "Uncle Mitch," who do nothing but "talk about trains and highways."

All images contained in this work are part of the Mitchell E. Dakelman collection unless noted otherwise.

INTRODUCTION

Our story begins in the early 1960s with two young boys who had never met. One grew up near Pittsburgh, the other in central New Jersey. I was the boy from Pittsburgh. One of the fondest memories of my childhood was our family trips to visit my uncle Sam in Richmond, Virginia. We would set off in our bright red 1959 Plymouth Fury with its huge fins and head east on the Pennsylvania Turnpike. The best part of the journey was always my father's sudden proclamation, "Tunnel! Tunnel!" as we approached the Laurel Hill and Allegheny Mountain Tunnels. Whether or not he knew a tunnel was ahead by virtue of one of the "Tunnel–1 Mile" signs or merely through familiarity with the highway, I will never know for sure.

Whatever the case, my younger brother and I would squeal with delight as we approached the tunnel. We were already aware that the tunnels were dark and narrow, and we would be subjected to the odor of noxious exhaust fumes and the roar of oncoming trucks passing just a few feet from our car. Being in the days when few cars had air-conditioning, we of course travelled with the windows down to deal with the summer heat. Knowing what was about to confront us, we quickly rolled up the back windows while our parents did the same in the front. It was always a harrowing experience to travel through the tunnels at that time, and I always felt a sense of relief once we exited the other end. Once more, our family had traversed one of those dimly lit Pennsylvania Turnpike tunnels with our lives intact!

The other boy, who would someday become my closest friend, was Mitchell Dakelman. Having grown up in New Jersey, Mitch was used to the New Jersey Turnpike with its six lanes, modern-looking overpasses, and state-of-the-art electronic warning signs. His first recollection of the Pennsylvania Turnpike dates to 1961 during a trip to Hershey Park. All of a sudden, he travelled on a highway very different than those back in New Jersey. Here was a quaint-looking road with just two lanes in each direction, a narrow median, and overpasses that looked like antiques. Many years later, I would ask Mitch what his initial impression was of the Pennsylvania Turnpike. He uttered but a single word: primitive.

In my own case, I was much more enamored of Pennsylvania Route 126 south of Breezewood, which was being converted to Interstate 70, a transformation I witnessed as we headed south to Richmond. The smooth concrete pavement and modern overpasses were far more inspiring than the rough asphalt and ancient-looking bridges of the Pennsylvania Turnpike.

Years would pass, and then as young adults, we would again travel the Pennsylvania Turnpike, but this time we were behind the wheel instead of in the back seat. From this vantage point, it became clear to both of us that this was not just some beat-up old highway. There was something very special and unique about it. Independently, we both began to research the road with the help of old maps, the few books available on the subject, and letters sent to the Pennsylvania Turnpike Commission seeking answers to our questions.

Still never having met, both of us eventually independently ventured out to Sideling and Rays Hill Tunnels just east of Breezewood. Both had been bypassed and abandoned in 1968. By the time we arrived there, the tunnels and adjoining roadway looked like something out of a movie set from *The Planet of the Apes*. For me, staring at the single-tube tunnel portals brought back childhood memories of travelling through those dank tunnels with my family on our way to Richmond. For Mitch, they gave him his first in-person look at an original single-bore tunnel that he never had the opportunity to see in service as a child.

In 1985, I wrote an article for the Train Collectors Association's publication, the *TCA Quarterly*, which described a model railroad I had built. The layout portrayed the South Pennsylvania Railroad. It was this unfinished railroad's abandoned roadbed upon which much of the turnpike would eventually be built. Mitch too was a member of the TCA, read the article, and tracked me down. I received a lengthy letter from him that ended to the effect that "we would probably be very good friends." How prophetic! I was thrilled to discover that there was at least one other person in this world who liked highways as much as I did. We eventually met in person, and in the years that followed, together we would explore the old South Penn right-of-way, share our highway research materials, and plan trips to look at highways.

Around 2002, we became aware of Arcadia's series of photo histories covering a huge range of topics. Drawing on Mitch's massive collection of historic turnpike photographs and my interest in highway engineering, we collaborated on the book *The Pennsylvania Turnpike*, published by Arcadia in 2004.

As the years passed, Mitch continued to collect archival photographs of the turnpike, and as the 75th anniversary of the highway approached in 2015, we began to discuss the possibility of doing a second book. After some initial hesitation, we decided to create a second volume, but one very different not just from our first book but the handful of others ever published on this subject.

We had two goals in mind with the creation of this book. The first was to present images of the turnpike in a large format, rather than the smaller images used in our prior book. The vast majority of these photographs are newly discovered and have never been published before in a general-distribution book.

The second is much more important. Just as the two of us as young boys viewed the turnpike as a worn and obsolete highway, so too did we recognize that that remains the perception of much of the motoring public today. The truth is that when the highway first opened, and for many years thereafter, it was a source of wonder and amazement to everyone who used it. It was a supreme engineering achievement, and it was a harbinger of the huge social changes that would impact our nation in the post–World War II era.

Unfortunately, with each passing day, the number of people who recall the turnpike in its glory years continues to dwindle. As such, in this book, we focus tightly on the original section of the turnpike between Irwin and Carlisle. Moreover, we tell the story of how the brand-new highway captured the imagination of the public, the road's fall from grace starting sometime in the 1950s, and the efforts made by the Pennsylvania Turnpike Commission since the turn of the 21st century to restore some of that lost glory. Those seeking a broader history of the highway are referred to our 2004 publication. Come along with us as we recall the glory days of the Pennsylvania Turnpike, and please enjoy the ride!

—Neal A. Schorr

OPPOSITE: A quarter-century after work ceased on the South Pennsylvania Railroad, its half-finished tunnels continued to be a source of public fascination. Although they gradually disappeared into the woods, rumors continued to circulate that the project would be revived. This is a postcard image of Tuscarora Tunnel. The post office cancellation on the back dates it to 1918 or earlier.

ONE

THE GHOST OF THE SOUTH PENN

Long before the Pennsylvania Turnpike was ever envisioned, railroads were the form of transportation that ruled the nation. Construction of the railroads began in the 1830s, the goal being to link the East Coast with the Ohio River. The first tracks were those of the Baltimore & Ohio Railroad (B&O). Eventually, railroad fever would sweep the nation, and the race was on to reach the Ohio River and points beyond. Nowhere was that battle more intensely waged than in the cities of New York, Philadelphia, and Baltimore, all of which were trying to become the railroad gateway to the West. It was the success of the earlier water-level Erie Canal, in striking contrast to the many problems of the Pennsylvania Mainline Canal, that was the source of this battle.

The Erie Canal traversed flat terrain and provided an easy means of navigation to the West. On the other hand, the Pennsylvania facility crossed the Appalachian Mountains. Often referred to as the "Endless Mountains," since one ridge seemed to follow another without end, they presented a formidable obstacle to any means of transportation across the commonwealth of Pennsylvania. Unlike the Erie Canal, the route across Pennsylvania had to be traversed by a cumbersome combination of canals and "inclined planes." These were short stretches of railroad where the canal boats were taken out of the water, placed on railroad cars, and hauled up the mountainsides by means of stationary steam engines. The facility was never particularly successful, and given this reality, the people of Philadelphia who backed the construction of a railroad across Pennsylvania were determined not to allow this to happen again.

In Maryland, the B&O pushed to the west, seeking a charter from the Pennsylvania State Legislature to traverse the southwest corner of Pennsylvania to reach the Ohio River. To the north, Cornelius Vanderbilt built his New York Central Railroad up the east shore of the Hudson River before turning west at Albany to reach Lake Erie. Not wanting to repeat the experience of the Pennsylvania Mainline Canal, the leaders of the city of Philadelphia pushed forward with a plan to construct a railroad across the commonwealth. Ultimately, the state legislature granted a charter for the construction of such a railroad. The charter

contained a specific provision stating that should the railroad be placed under construction before the B&O could enter Pennsylvania, the charter of the B&O would be lifted.

The commonwealth commissioned a survey to determine how best to route the new railroad across Pennsylvania. Col. Charles Schlatter was hired to conduct this survey and devised three routes. One went far to the north and was quite circuitous. A route to the south was the shortest of the three but had the steepest grades. The route in between the other two followed the Juniata River Valley to the base of the Alleghenies. From there, it ascended the mountains. After much study, the middle route was chosen for the new railroad.

Work on the Pennsylvania Railroad (Pennsy) began in 1846, and with the completion of the Horseshoe Curve in 1854, the commonwealth was finally spanned by a modern, competitive railroad. Over the next half-century, the Pennsy expanded aggressively through the acquisition of other railroads. Eventually, it would become the largest railroad in the country and one of the largest corporations in the nation.

To the north, Vanderbilt's New York Central Railroad flourished as well and grew to be Pennsy's fiercest competitor. Not willing to concede any business to the New York Central, the Pennsy began to construct the West Shore Railroad on the western bank of the Hudson River, across the river from the NYC's main line. Enraged, Vanderbilt's son William, now head of the New York Central, began to provide funding for a railroad that would span south-central Pennsylvania. The railroad would be built on Schlatter's southern route and would come to be named the South Pennsylvania Railroad (South Penn).

The South Penn had been envisioned earlier, but lacking adequate funding, the only work ever performed on the route was the grading of a few miles of roadbed near the eastern terminus. The goal was to connect the Reading Railroad to the east with Pittsburgh to the west and to provide a shorter and more competitive route to Pittsburgh than the Pennsy. With funding from Vanderbilt, as well as Pittsburgh steel magnate Andrew Carnegie, now in place, work could now proceed at a rapid pace. In 1883, thousands of workers poured into the woods of southern Pennsylvania to construct the railroad. Work began to grade many miles of roadbed, and stone culverts were constructed to carry the fill of the South Penn over numerous streams. More importantly, work began on nine tunnels that would pierce the Endless Mountains. Schlatter's survey was performed with uncanny skill, and he was able to locate the tunnels such that they struck the mountain ridges at right angles, strengthening their bores and thereby keeping their length to a minimum.

Over the next two years, work continued at a steady pace. The project did not escape the notice of the financier J.P. Morgan. He recognized that both the South Penn and the West Shore Railroad would duplicate the existing main lines of the Pennsy and the New York Central, respectively. This battle between the two railroad giants would be self-destructive to both. Accordingly, in the summer of 1885, Morgan arranged for a meeting between Vanderbilt and Pennsylvania Railroad president George P. Roberts on his yacht, The Corsair. Morgan pointed out the futility of this war and forged a deal between the two railroads. Vanderbilt would cease all work on the South Penn, and in return, the Pennsy would turn over control of the West Shore to the New York Central.

With the deal being done, work ceased on the South Penn almost immediately. The workers who had poured into the woods of southern Pennsylvania two years earlier simply walked off the job. Picks and shovels were left where they were last used, and miles and miles of partially graded roadbed were left to Mother Nature. More importantly, nine partially bored tunnels were left to excite the imagination of those who sought a route through the mountains of southern Pennsylvania.

By the time the project was abandoned, over 60 percent of the work had been completed. No other railroad in American history came as close to completion as the South Penn without actually ever having been finished. Multiple attempts were made to revive the project over the next half-century. Not a single one succeeded. Over the next 50 years, the right-of-way would largely be forgotten, hidden away in the woods of southern Pennsylvania.

This is one of a series of images taken during the initial turnpike survey conducted in 1936–1937. They were obtained from a private collection rather than a public source. The image likely was taken from Rays Hill looking to the west, with Aliquippa Gap seen in the distance.

Much of the South Penn's route passed through pastoral farm valleys such as the one in this survey image. This part of the route was relatively easy to construct.

This survey image provides an idea of the challenges faced by the South Penn, as well as the proposed new highway. The terrain consisted of one mountain ridge after another, hence the origin of the expression "the Endless Mountains." They were a significant barrier to any means of transportation. Although the precise location is unknown, the appearance of the ridge suggests it is along the eastern half of the route.

Here is a postcard view taken from Bill's Place, which was a mere speck on the map along the Lincoln Highway a few miles east of Breezewood. The location is at the top of Rays Hill. A partially bored South Penn tunnel pierced the ridge not far from this location.

After half a century, most of the South Penn right-of-way had disappeared into the woods of south central Pennsylvania. Trees and underbrush have almost completely obscured the right-of-way in this view taken by the survey crew.

In some cases, the abandoned right-of-way found a second life as a path or trail. Here, some of the vegetation has been cleared, and there is evidence of passing wheeled vehicles.

Sometimes, the right-of-way was clearly visible, such as in this image. The precise location is unknown.

A small section of the South Penn right-of-way a few miles west of Somerset was eventually put to use as a logging railroad. It was named the Pittsburgh, Westmoreland & Somerset (PW&S). The railroad completed Quemahoning Tunnel and laid tracks along a section of the abandoned South Penn right-of-way. The railroad was chartered in 1899 and abandoned in 1917. The presence of railroad ties in this image suggests that this was a section of the South Penn utilized by the PW&S.

The survey crews also evaluated the nine South Penn tunnels for potential vehicular use. They found the portals to be in varying stages of completion, though aside from Quemahoning, none of the tunnels were bored through. Most resembled little more than naturally occurring caves. This is a view of the western portal of Kittatinny Mountain Tunnel. The image is extremely unique since unlike most photographs of the partially bored tunnels, here the South Penn right-of-way can clearly be seen approaching the tunnel portal from a considerable distance. Furthermore, the use of the right-of-way by motorized vehicles is obvious.

Here is a view of the western portal of Rays Hill Tunnel. Identification of both the east and west portals of this tunnel is possible since both had some cribbing installed near the mouth of the tunnel. The survey crews have installed a "No Trespassing" sign, which is barely visible in the center of the tunnel heading.

In some of the tunnels, work had begun on lining them with stone, as is evident near the left of the image. The shape of the rock near the top of the bore identifies this as being the eastern portal of Kittatinny Mountain Tunnel.

At other sites, work had actually begun on the stone portals. Several courses of stone remained to be put into place at this site. This is the eastern end of Blue Mountain Tunnel. Identification is made easy by comparing this to known photographs of this portal showing the same level of completion and the two protruding rocks above and just to the right of the keystone. Compare this to the image of the fully completed portal at Tuscarora Mountain Tunnel on page nine.

As with the tunnel portals, the tunnel interiors reached various levels of completion. In this bore, no work has yet begun on the tunnel lining. In contrast, all of the tunnels were partially flooded, since the portals became obstructed by rock slides.

In this tunnel, not only have some of the stone walls been completed, but so has a portion of the arch. While the location is unknown, the state of completion suggests that this is either Tuscarora or Blue Mountain Tunnel.

Quemahoning was the only tunnel to have been bored through, and as such, it received a complete lining. However, in contrast to the work performed by the South Penn, this tunnel was lined with timbers, a much less expensive proposition. It too was flooded at the time of the initial turnpike survey.

OPPOSITE: The Bronx River Parkway was the first express highway built in America. Most of the crossroads were grade separated, as in this image. At this early date, the road was not yet divided. Building on the success of this road, more of these express highways would be built around New York City.

TWO

DREAMING OF A SUPERHIGHWAY

A half-century after the abandonment of the South Penn, a new form of transportation had evolved that would signal the eventual end of the railroad as the dominant form of transportation in this country. That of course was the automobile. Having its origins near the beginning of the 20th century, by the 1920s, the automobile was clogging the streets of America's cities. Growing more powerful and sophisticated as the years passed, all that was missing were modern highways that would allow the automobile to achieve its full potential.

Perhaps the earliest attempt to create such a road was the construction of the Bronx River Parkway north of New York City. Completed in 1925, this roadway could be considered the world's first express highway, the term used at the time for what would today be known as an expressway. While lacking a divider separating opposing traffic and having several at-grade intersections, this road presaged what was to come. Gradually, more of these express highways were built in and around New York City, culminating with the opening of Connecticut's Merritt Parkway in 1938.

Similar efforts were undertaken in Europe, though with a sinister motive in mind. In the

1930s, Adolph Hitler began constructing his own expressways across Germany, ostensibly to serve the German motoring public but, in fact, as part of his preparation for war. Known as autobahns, these roads would prove to be invaluable to the German military during the Second World War.

Although work had stopped on the South Penn in 1885, the dream of completing the railroad never died. Even as late as the early 20th century, efforts were still being made to complete the line. In 1933, Edward H. Flinkinger, then chief of city planning in the Pennsylvania Department of Internal Affairs, set out to explore the abandoned South Penn right-of-way in the Path Valley, just as he did as a youth. As a boy, he played on the old right-of-way and explored the unfinished tunnels. While examining his childhood playground, he envisioned the old roadbed and tunnels being completed as a new express highway linking Harrisburg with Pittsburgh. When he returned to Harrisburg, he approached Norman Stiteler, an official of the Portland Cement Association, who in turn spoke with Sidney Snow and Victor Lecoq. Both were with the Pennsylvania State Planning Commission. They received support from William H. Sutherland, general manager for the Pennsylvania Motor Trucking Association.

After a new political administration entered office in 1935, Lecoq and Sutherland approached state legislator Cliff Patterson, who supported their idea. He believed the project would give Pennsylvania an economic shot in the arm, provide needed employment, and help the work-starved construction industry. Patterson introduced a resolution asking the legislature and senate to investigate the project's feasibility on April 23, 1935.

Although state funds were unavailable for a survey, a grant was received through the Works Progress Administration (WPA). Throughout 1936 and 1937, a survey was made of the proposed right-of-way by the Pennsylvania Department of Highways, including the extant portions of the South Penn. Traffic studies along the proposed highway's parallel roads were conducted to see if the project could be justified.

After a report indicating that the project was feasible was made available to the legislature based on the survey's findings, Gov. George H. Earle signed into law on May 21, 1937, Bill 211, creating the Pennsylvania Turnpike Commission. The job of the commission would to be construct a new express highway through the mountains using the South Penn right-of-way. Unfortunately, the legislation failed to provide funding for the project. Therefore, the first job of the commission was to obtain the financing to construct the new 160-mile-long highway.

Earle had appointed businessman Walter A. Jones of Pittsburgh as the chairman of the commission. His first task was to obtain the estimated $50 million needed to build the highway. Under his direction, the commission attempted to float bonds to finance the project. Unfortunately, given the financial realities of the Depression, as well as the fear of investors that no one would use a toll road in the middle of nowhere, the effort failed, and the bond offering was withdrawn.

Jones, being well connected in Washington, was able to interest Pres. Franklin Roosevelt in the project. With war clouds gathering in Europe and recognizing the highway's potential military value in time of war, he lent his support to the project. Through the Reconstruction Finance Corporation and the Public Works Administration (PWA), Roosevelt helped to secure the money necessary to fund the construction of the nation's first long-distance superhighway. In 1938, the PWA granted $29.25 million, and the Pennsylvania Turnpike Commission sold $40 million worth of bonds to the Reconstruction Finance Corporation. Vanderbilt's half-finished tunnels would at last see the light of day, though in a manner that he never could have imagined.

With the passage of time, the design of the new express highways grew more sophisticated. This is an image of the Belt Parkway near New York City. By the late 1930s, when this highway was designed, opposing traffic was separated by a grass median. The attention to aesthetics was obvious, with the stone-faced overpass and the decorative light poles. The low height of the overpass was chosen to limit use of the parkways to automobiles. Trucks were simply too tall to pass under the bridges.

The old South Penn bores had to be assessed in order to determine if they could be converted to vehicular use. Part of the work of the 1936–1937 survey crew was to make the tunnels accessible so that they could be cleared, then drained. This rare "unofficial" image is one of a series believed to have been taken by a member of the survey crew and was eventually acquired by a private collector. It shows an access road that has been cleared, allowing motorized vehicles to access a tunnel portal.

This is Sideling Hill Tunnel following initial clearing. Water that had been trapped in the tunnel is seen draining down the rutted access road.

Here is another image from the same privately held collection. After access was obtained, heavy equipment was brought in to completely clear the portals. This allowed the tunnels to be fully drained prior to being assessed. The crude access road to the portal was cleared sufficiently to allow the passage of not just heavy equipment, but rubber-tired vehicles as well. This is a view of Gunter's Valley between Kittatinny and Blue Mountain Tunnels.

This is the same general view as the prior photograph, but the image was part of the "official" survey, as indicated by the words "Pennsylvania Department of Highways Photo" in the lower right corner. Pipes brought in to be used in the drainage efforts can be seen in the center of the photograph. Some of the original stone lining of the tunnel is visible in the lower left corner.

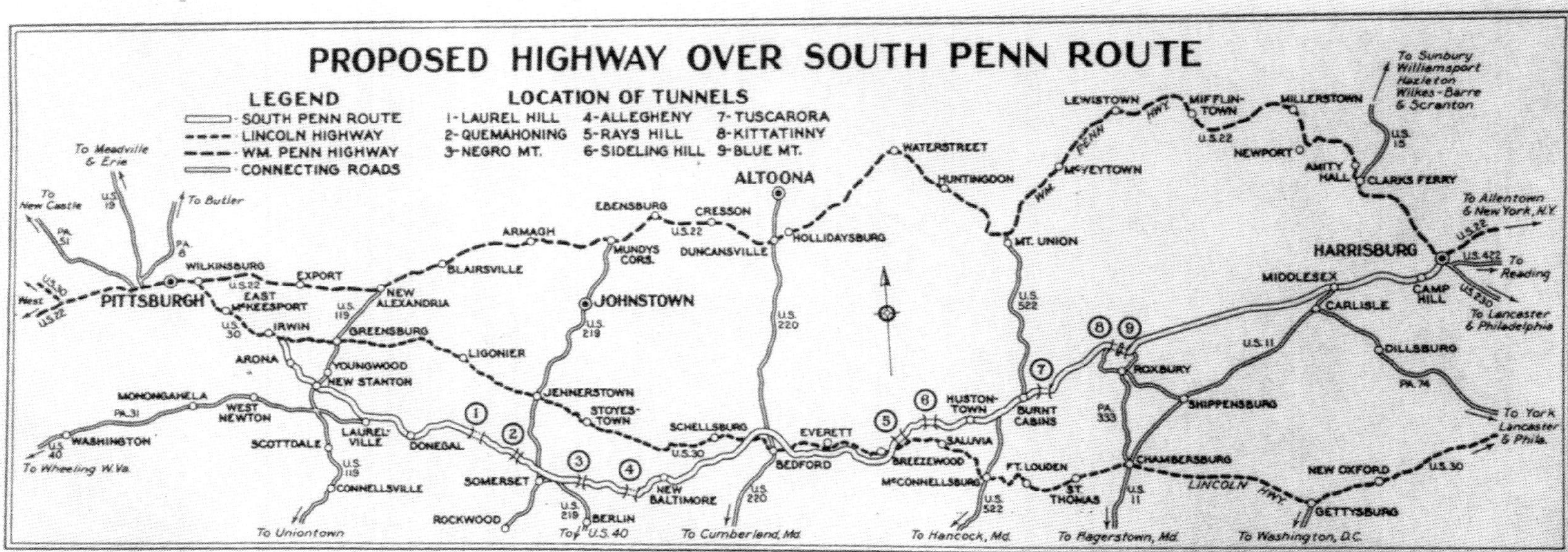

The survey of 1936–1937 suggested that it was indeed possible to utilize the roadbed and tunnels of the South Penn to construct a new "all-weather" highway through the mountains. At this point, the Pennsylvania Turnpike Commission began to develop specific proposals and to promote the idea to the public and potential funding sources. Among its efforts was this map of a proposed route that utilized all nine South Penn tunnels. When actually built, Quemahoning and Negro Mountain Tunnels were bypassed.

This is an early promotional display created by the Philadelphia Museum Extension Project of the WPA. While indicating that the project was "now under construction," the display contains multiple errors. First, the map near the top indicates that the new road would utilize all nine South Penn bores. The rendering depicts sequential tunnels suggestive of Blue and Kittatinny Mountain Tunnels, but in reality, the small ridge between the two mountains does not exist. The portal looks nothing like the real structure, and the image shows a four-lane tunnel, when in fact it would have only two lanes.

A subsequent artist's rendering is only marginally more accurate. The number of lanes has been correctly reduced to two, and the concentric rings of the portal bear a vague resemblance to what was actually constructed. But the Colonial-style fan house above the portal is pure fantasy.

This large promotional display is particularly noteworthy, as it contains historical images of the South Penn while under construction, as well as erroneous and accurate renderings of the new highway. Just to the left of center is the image presented on the prior page. At the very center is a different tunnel rendering that, though not completely accurate, more closely captures the final appearance of the new tunnels. In contrast, the rendering at bottom center of one of the turnpike's rigid-frame concrete-arch bridges passing over the new highway is exceptionally accurate.

This is the drawing seen at the bottom center of the display on the preceding page. Here, the artist has accurately illustrated the masonry detail work as used in the parapets and wing walls. Furthermore, the depiction of the guardrails and the proportion of the median width to the traffic lanes is all correct. The only bit of artistic license is the shrubs planted in the median. At last, the public was provided with an accurate image of what would soon come to pass.

Opposite: With the awarding of construction contracts, thousands of workers poured into the woods of south central Pennsylvania, just as they had a half-century earlier with the start of work on the South Penn. The area was a remote wilderness, so construction camps such as this were established to house the workers. The photographer and location are unknown, and the image is part of another privately held collection documenting the work on the turnpike.

THREE

BUILDING THE WORLD'S GREATEST HIGHWAY

With funding now secured, work could begin on the project. Though much of the right-of-way had not yet been purchased, the first contract was awarded on October 26, 1938, and ground-breaking occurred in Cumberland County the very next day. The commission was charged with the difficult task of getting the road completed by May 1, 1940, later extended to June 29. Workers began to pour into the woods of southern Pennsylvania as they had with the South Penn half a century earlier. Just as on the South Penn, work camps were established to house them. Unlike the workers on the South Penn, who relied on picks, shovels, and black powder, the men building the Pennsylvania Turnpike were able to avail themselves of modern construction equipment never dreamed of 50 years earlier.

But the more important advance was in the design of the highway. While express highways had been around since the Bronx River Parkway, none had ever been built through such rugged territory or to such a high engineering standard. The final design called for four 12-foot lanes separated by a 10-foot grass median. Stabilized 10-foot-wide shoulders were incorporated into the design as well. All crossroads would be grade separated, and access would be limited, provided only at 11 interchanges. Ramps leading to and from these interchanges would be provided with acceleration and deceleration lanes of exceptional length for the time. More importantly, and unlike other express highways built up to this time, these standards would be consistently adhered to along the entire length of the turnpike.

Work got under way grading the route with modern earth-moving equipment. The best

example of the extent of this work occurred near Everett. Here, a huge fill was constructed to carry the new highway over State Route 26. Just to the east was Clear Ridge Cut. At 153 feet in depth, it was one of the deepest cuts in the United States and was used rather than a tunnel, as was originally envisioned.

One of the most important tasks facing the construction crews was the work needed to make the South Penn bores suitable for vehicular use. Although the South Penn route included nine tunnels, it was decided to bypass Quemahoning and Negro Mountain Tunnels. When the initial feasibility studies were conducted a few years before the start of construction, the mouths of the tunnels had been largely obliterated by rock slides. The effect was that of a dam, thereby partially filling the tunnels with water. Later, the portals were cleared and the water drained to assess the viability of the tunnels for vehicular use. Aside from Quemahoning Tunnel, which was briefly used by the Pittsburgh, Westmoreland & Somerset Railroad, none of the other tunnels had ever been completely bored through.

As such, the first order of business was to not only finish boring the tunnels but to enlarge them to accommodate two lanes of traffic. The tunnels were then lined with concrete, portals constructed at either end, and ventilation provisions installed. The most brilliant lighting available at the time was selected, in this case mercury vapor illumination.

Many bridges and culverts were required, both to serve crossroads and span watercourses. Three basic bridge types were used to carry local roads over the turnpike. These included the through steel girder and cast-in-place concrete T-beam bridges with a center pier. The third type was the rigid-frame concrete-arch bridges that were built in several different architectural styles. Aside from the seven tunnels, they were the signature item of the new road.

As work progressed, paving operations got under way. Forms were placed at the pavement edge, and the concrete was poured directly on the compacted-earth base, which was standard practice at the time. Once poured, workers finished the concrete slabs by hand, then the slabs were covered with wet burlap until they cured. Joints were later sealed after the curing process was complete.

Once paving was finished, final grading of the median and stabilization of the shoulders was completed. Next, guardrails, signage, and the turnpike's distinctive "cat's eye" reflectors were installed. The final step was the application of pavement markings. After almost two years of construction, the turnpike was at last ready for motorists.

The initial work consisted of excavating hillsides and ridgetops. This image is believed to show the work in Aliquippa Gap on the face of Tussey Mountain. This is just west of Everett. An excavating machine can be seen at the very center of the photograph.

This is an extremely rare panoramic view taken of the excavation work on the turnpike in Aliquippa Gap. In the center of the picture, the face of Tussey Mountain has been blasted away. An excavating machine can be seen just to the left of center. To the left of it is a lineup of equipment used to haul away the excavated rock. A local road would utilize the upper ledge where the excavating equipment is located. The turnpike would be built on the lower ledge. The river coursing across the image is the Raystown Branch of the Juniata River. The Lincoln Highway (US Route 30) can be seen in the lower right corner. The railroad bridge connecting the State Line Branch of the Pennsylvania Railroad to the Huntingdon & Broad Top Mountain Railroad is visible just above where Route 30 curves behind the trees.

This is a close-up view of one of the excavating machines used to load blasted rock into dump trucks to be hauled away and used for fill elsewhere along the route of the turnpike. Nello Teer was the name of one of the contractors hired by the Pennsylvania Turnpike Commission to build the new highway.

In some cases, excavated rock was loaded into tracked equipment such as this. It was then hauled away by bulldozers.

After the heavy excavation work was completed, scrapers pulled by bulldozers were used to form the right-of-way. This brought it close to the final shape needed to construct the highway.

This is a wider-angle shot of the bottom of a deep cut, as evidenced by the shadow visible across the bottom of the image. Note the shadows of the two onlookers near the bottom right corner of the picture. The photograph was taken near Everett and shows the broad expanse of the right-of-way and a different type of scraper than seen in the previous image.

Somewhat further along in the process, the right-of-way begins to assume its final shape. In the very center of the image, a fill has been constructed to span a small valley using material excavated out of the adjoining cuts. Along the horizon, crews can be seen excavating Clear Ridge Cut, one of the deepest in the United States at the time. The image was taken at Earlston, a small town adjacent to Everett.

This is another view of grading operations, this one taken many miles to the east in the Path Valley. A bridge over a local road is present in the center of the image. Amberson Mountain, which splits the valley in two, can be seen in the distance. The turnpike veered off to the right into the Amberson Valley. The farm structures to the right of the bridge and the double-masted utility pole to the left all still exist today.

Beyond grading the right-of-way, the biggest task facing the commission was the boring through and completion of the seven South Penn tunnels to be used for the turnpike. What is remarkable about this photograph is that as late as July 1939, the date appearing in the lower left corner of the image, work had yet to begin on some of the tunnels. In less than 15 months, this tunnel would be holed through and converted for vehicular use, a truly incredible feat!

Before work could begin on the tunnels, a staging area had to be created near the tunnel portals. This is a view of the western portal of Allegheny Mountain Tunnel taken on July 25, 1939. The photograph was taken by Jean Schwartz, who performed much of the commission's photography.

After clearing the staging area, excavating crews would fully clear the portal area of debris to allow unobstructed access to the tunnel. This is a postcard view of the eastern end of Sideling Hill Tunnel.

With the portal area cleared, tunnel crews could now turn their attention to clearing the tunnel itself and finishing the boring work left uncompleted by the South Penn. In this view of the west end of Rays Hill Tunnel, significant amounts of debris can be seen within the tunnel. One of the "No Trespassing" signs erected during the survey of 1936–1937 is still in place. The image was taken by turnpike photographer Jean Schwartz on September 26, 1939.

In order to prevent collapse of the unreinforced portals, temporary shoring was sometimes used. This is an image of the western end of Sideling Hill Tunnel.

Next, tracks were installed so that small mine cars could haul rock out of the tunnels as crews completed boring and enlarging the tunnel. This is a view of the western portal of Laurel Hill Tunnel, and a considerable amount of shoring has been put in place.

This unusual view was taken from atop the eastern portal of Kittatinny Mountain Tunnel looking toward Blue Mountain Tunnel. The two tunnels were separated by just a few hundred feet. Temporary tracks and mine cars are plainly visible. A concrete batch plant is off to the right, and forms have now been erected to create the concrete tunnel portal. A temporary bridge spans the stream in Gunters Valley at the bottom of the image.

Here, forms used to construct the concrete tunnel lining have been erected at the eastern portal of Blue Mountain Tunnel. The large pipes drain water that has seeped into the tunnel from cracks and fissures in the rock.

In this view near the west end of Kittatinny Tunnel, the forms have been extended into the bore prior to pumping in the concrete that will create the tunnel lining. The excavating crews have struck a vein of water-saturated sand, which has collapsed into the tunnel and obstructed the bore. It had to be cleared and the excavation stabilized before work could resume.

This is an extremely unusual view of the precast drain pipe that would be installed in the floor of the tunnel underneath the roadway. The pipe would drain water brought in by vehicles and that which seeped from rock through the concrete tunnel lining. The unique appearance of the Cold Spring Road Bridge in the background clearly identifies this as the western portal of Kittatinny Mountain Tunnel. The picture was obtained from a privately held collection.

As work proceeded within the tunnel, crews started to build the concrete portals at both ends. This photograph was taken at the western end of Laurel Hill Tunnel by Jack Pletcher, another photographer who documented the construction of the turnpike. More of the precast concrete drain pipe may be seen in the lower left corner of the image.

Here, most of the concrete portal has been completed, and work is now under way on the fan house atop the structure. It housed two large fans used to clear vehicle exhaust fumes from the tunnel. The photograph was taken by Jean Schwartz on June 6, 1940, at the eastern end of Sideling Hill Tunnel.

This is another view of the eastern end of Sideling Hill taken later that summer. With the fan house completed, crews next installed the stainless steel trim around the backlit sign that would proclaim the name of the tunnel. The concrete pavement is also now evident.

Here are two of a series of photographs taken of Kittatinny Mountain Tunnel. The above image clearly reveals some of the tunnel's architectural details. Its distinctive concentric concrete arches are plainly visible and represent an architectural touch that would stand the test of time. While brick facing was considered early in the planning process, the commission opted for a less expensive design that emphasized the horizontal form marks. In the below image, one of the construction workers poses for the photographer. A gate has been installed to keep out the curious, who have already been attracted to the project even before its opening.

These are images of the western end of Tuscarora Mountain Tunnel. The above photograph is dated September 30, 1940, the day before the turnpike opened. This is clearly an error given the amount of incomplete work. Pavement markings have yet to be painted, light poles are not yet installed, and temporary electric lines are still in place. Furthermore, the irregularly spaced lights within the tunnel suggest they are temporary fixtures. By contrast, the postcard image below shows the tunnel fully completed and ready for service.

Aside from the tunnels, the signature item of the new highway would be the rigid-frame concrete-arch bridges. These were built of reinforced concrete. In order to construct the bridge, wooden forms were first erected, then steel rebars were shaped and placed inside the forms. Finally, the concrete was poured. Once the concrete was cured, the forms were stripped off the new bridge. This structure was located in Donegal Township within Westmoreland County and was photographed on May 8, 1940, by Jean Schwartz.

There were a few variations of the rigid-frame concrete-arch bridges, and the type shown here was the most common of the genre. The distinctive features are the decorative parapets and the angled wing walls. Part of the motivation in building such ornate parapets was to create work for concrete masons near the end of the Great Depression. This structure was located a few miles west of Tuscarora Mountain Tunnel and was photographed on September 9, 1940, by Jean Schwartz.

Shown here are the two other variations of the rigid-frame arch bridges. The structure in the above photograph has wing walls that are parallel to the bridge, and the parapet is carried onto them. These were typically used in cuts. The bridge in the photograph below was less common; it had solid rather than open parapets and lacked the concrete towers at either end of the arch. These too were photographed by Jean Schwartz in September 1940. They were part of the Pennsylvania Turnpike Commission's efforts to photographically document all of the bridges before the highway opened on October 1. The upper structure was in Westmoreland County, and the lower was in Somerset County.

The turnpike also used steel through girder bridges to carry local roads over the new highway. They were strictly functional and had much less aesthetic appeal than the rigid-frame concrete-arch bridges. This type of bridge can be seen in the following series of photographs, which were all recorded west of the Fort Littleton interchange. The newly completed US Route 522 bridge can be seen in the above image. Just below it is a small work camp. But the unique feature of this photograph is the steel plate girder resting on the truck and bulldozer at left in the image. Its destination is uncertain, but it likely is headed to the construction site shown in the below image. That image shows the Davis Lane Bridge, which was located about two miles west of the US 522 structure. One of the two main girders is already in place. Both images were obtained from a privately held collection.

Moving a few miles farther west, the Little Egypt Road bridge crosses over the turnpike near Hiram. Unlike the two prior images, this was taken by Jean Schwartz shortly before the turnpike opened. This structure was located on a section of the turnpike that would be abandoned in 1968 with the opening of the Sideling/Rays Hill bypass. The structure remained in service over the unused highway for many years but was eventually torn down and replaced by an earthen fill.

The third and least common type of bridge was the center-pier concrete T-beam bridges. These were poured in place, as were the rigid-frame arch bridges. They were used early in the construction process and were built only west of Breezewood. Their use was discontinued when it became apparent that their center pier was a safety hazard. Because of the use of non-air-entrained concrete in their construction, they deteriorated relatively quickly, and none survived past the 1990s. This structure was located near Ashcom.

This view shows two bridges in close proximity near Husband. The foreground structure is another example of a concrete T-beam bridge. Its right-hand span frames a rare steel through girder bridge with a center pier. There were only three of these on the entire turnpike, and only two had this particular design. The two structures seen in this image were replaced by a single structure that opened in 2015. It would be located halfway between the two.

Only one structure carried a rail line above the turnpike. It was located near Hecla Road, a few miles east of New Stanton. The bridge carried the tracks of West Penn Railways, a local interurban line. The system was abandoned in the early 1950s, but the bridge would stand for roughly a decade before it was dismantled. This is another image created by Jean Schwartz and is dated September 13, 1940, just two weeks before the turnpike opened to traffic.

The area of Pennsylvania traversed by the turnpike was relatively desolate, and at the time the highway opened, few if any roadside services were available at the exits. Therefore, the commission constructed service plazas at intervals of about 30 miles. They provided food, fuel, and restroom facilities to travelers. They were built of Pennsylvania quarry stone reflective of early Pennsylvania Colonial architecture. Initially, all but one were small structures with limited dining facilities, such as this one under construction at New Baltimore.

The one exception was the South Midway service plaza, seen at left in the image above, near Bedford. So named because it was located at the midpoint of the turnpike, it was the flagship of the service plazas. It was a magnificent structure that included a full-service restaurant run by the Howard Johnson's chain, as well as a truckers' dormitory. The structure was located directly across from the diminutive North Midway plaza, as can be seen in this aerial view. A pedestrian tunnel was built underneath the turnpike so that westbound travelers could access the restaurant.

Toll collection facilities had to be constructed as well. This is an image of the facility at Carlisle looking toward the west. Since this and its counterpart at Irwin spanned the main line of the turnpike, they needed to have multiple exit and entry lanes. Those at the intermediate interchanges were smaller, having just one lane in each direction. The Carlisle tollbooth was built on top of a fill and had an elaborate foundation, as can be seen in the below image. Once completed, it would be faced with pale blue and yellow metal panels, the official colors of the commonwealth of Pennsylvania. It would last only until 1950, when the Philadelphia extension was opened. Both images are from a privately held collection.

This is the tollbooth at Irwin, the other end of the turnpike. It was the largest such structure on the road. The reason for the disparity in the number of lanes compared to the Carlisle interchange is unknown. The facility was referred to as a "ticket office" when the highway first opened. The photographer is standing on the ramps to and from westbound US Route 30, and the view is to the east. The precise date is unknown, but with the structure being nearly complete, the photograph was likely taken within a few weeks of opening day.

If the photographer who took the previous image turned around, this is what he would have seen. Shown is the site of the ramps that will connect the turnpike to US Route 30 in Irwin. Rough grading is complete, and final grading of the off ramp to westbound Route 30 appears to be finished. The ramp was unusual in that it crossed a local road before the merge point with Route 30. The image also reveals that Route 30 was a divided highway by that time.

This is another image showing the completed grading operations at the Fort Littleton interchange. The skewed US Route 522 bridge can barely be made out in the distance. Final compaction and smoothing of the graded base is all that needs to be completed prior to the start of paving operations.

The process of preparing the roadbed for paving is a little further along in this image. Here, the base has been compacted and stakes placed indicating the location of forms that will be used in the paving process. Note the inlet (drain) at the base of the cut near the left side of the image. It was built to remove water that drains into the cut. The photograph is dated 1939 and was taken looking westbound from the vicinity of the Diehl Road bridge near Mann's Choice.

The above image shows one of many batch plants that were placed along the length of the project. Here, the gravel, sand, and cement used in the concrete were stockpiled, then mixed together. The mixture was then trucked to the site of the paving operation as seen in the below photograph. The dry mix was dumped into receiving hoppers, which were then raised to an upright position. Next, the mixture dropped into a mixing machine, where it was combined with water. The wet concrete was placed in a bucket suspended from a boom arm and positioned over the paving machine, which rode on the forms seen in the lower left corner of the image. Finally, it was dropped between the forms so that it could be spread mechanically, then finished by hand. Railroad access to the project was limited, and the presence of the two tracks at right in the image above suggests that it was taken in the vicinity of either Bedford or New Stanton, both areas being served by branches of the Pennsylvania Railroad.

As with all of the work on the turnpike, the locals were intrigued by the work in progress. One of the greatest images taken by photographer Jack Pletcher is this one of a young boy who has ridden his bike to get a close-up view of the paving operations in progress. The photograph was taken on the grade west of Laurel Hill Tunnel leading to the turnpike's highest point.

This photograph was taken on a long uphill straightaway a few miles east of the Donegal interchange. A paving machine followed by a string of men finishing the wet concrete can be seen halfway up the left-hand concrete strip. This was one of the steepest tangents on the turnpike. A rigid-frame concrete-arch bridge is located at the summit.

This is one of the finest images ever recorded of paving operations on the turnpike. The location is the uphill grade from New Baltimore to Allegheny Mountain Tunnel. The machine that mixes the concrete is to the right of center. Its outstretched arm, suspending the bucket that would drop the concrete into the forms, is plainly visible. To its left are a paving machine and a group of workers who would finish the surface of the slab by hand. Dowel bars that reinforce the transverse joint can be seen at the extreme right of the photograph.

A few miles to the west, paving operations have been completed. A batch plant is visible just beyond the bridge. Scaffolding is in place to allow the construction crews to finish work on the abutments. This was among the sharpest curves on the turnpike and was necessary to keep the grade ascending Allegheny Mountain to no more than three percent.

Although the mainline of the turnpike was built of concrete, the ramps were constructed of asphalt. This image shows the on ramp at Carlisle as it headed to the toll both that spanned the highway. This ramp was closed when the turnpike was extended to Valley Forge, and traffic was diverted to what was originally known as the Middlesex interchange.

Sometimes, the turnpike had to reconstruct intersecting local roads. Such was the case at Carlisle Springs Road (Pennsylvania State Route 34). The reconstructed road was built of concrete, as evidenced by the forms, and the concrete-arch bridge carrying the turnpike over the highway can be seen in the distance.

By the late summer of 1940, paving operations were nearing completion, and most of the overpasses had been finished. This view was taken on the 12-mile-long "Straightaway" between the Blue Mountain and Carlisle exits. The next step would be to stabilize the median and shoulders.

A little later in the summer, the road was deemed sufficiently complete to allow a battalion of the Pennsylvania National Guard to conduct exercises on the new highway. This publicity photograph's caption reads that the "108th Field Artillery . . . made a 135-mile dash from Indiantown Gap, PA, to Bedford to 'save' the town from 'enemy attacks.' " The location was given as Bedford County, and the date was August 7, 1940.

This is another image of the same military exercise. Here, the caravan passes through Clear Ridge Cut and under the Ritchey Road bridge. Being amongst the deepest highway cuts in the United States at the time, it was always a point of photographic interest. It is unknown if the photographer seen at right was a member of the construction crew or simply a local who was aware of the maneuvers.

After the concrete roadway was poured, the next step was to stabilize the shoulders and build up and seed the median. Then the innovative skirt-type guardrail was installed. In that era, guardrails were typically constructed of steel cables mounted on wooden posts. The metal panels of the turnpike's guardrail were designed to deflect errant vehicles back onto the highway. The panels were blocked out so that out-of-control vehicles sliding along the panels would not snag on the posts. This scene was photographed about a mile east of Laurel Hill Tunnel.

The next step was to install the signage and reflective markers. The exit signs were given a bit of artistic flair with their stylized exit numbers, and the use of reflectors embedded within the demountable letters made them legible at night. The "cat's eye" reflectors were mounted in the median and at the edge of the shoulder. They consisted of six glass beads mounted in an elongated octagonal metal plate. Though a minor detail, they were one of the turnpike's signature items.

While the extent of the public's fascination with the new highway once it opened could not be foreseen, its significance as a civil engineering milestone was not lost on the Pennsylvania Turnpike Commission. Throughout the course of the project, photographers such as Jean Schwartz and Jack Pletcher documented the work. Here, a photographer creates an image of the massive fill over Pennsylvania State Route 26 with Clear Ridge Cut in the distance.

Here is a superb example of the photographer's work taken less than a month before the turnpike would open. This is an almost surreal view of the diminutive Cove Valley service plaza. While the structure is complete, the gas pumps in place, and the Esso sign erected, the people and the vehicles are all missing. In less than a month, it would be bustling with turnpike travelers and their cars and trucks and would eventually become one of the most photographed plazas on the new highway. The facility was just east of Sideling Hill Tunnel, and the mountain itself looms above the plaza in the background.

With less than a month to go before opening day, Jean Schwartz recorded this photograph of the US Route 522 bridge near Fort Littleton. Only two pieces of work remain to be completed. The small field office seen near the right-hand abutment will need to be dismantled, and the pavement markings will have to be applied. Once those tasks were completed, the road would be ready for use. Compare this photograph to the image on the top of page 57.

Some aerial photographs were taken of the turnpike shortly before it opened. This is a view of the western terminus with US Route 30 at Irwin. Careful study of the image reveals a number of unusual details. Both ramps carrying traffic to and from Pittsburgh (lower right corner) are two lanes wide. Local roads intersect the two shorter ramps exactly where they meet US Route 30 eastbound. Even more surprising, another local road, Penny Lane, literally cuts across the off ramp to Pittsburgh. Due to safety concerns, it would eventually be closed, but incredibly, that would not occur until 2002!

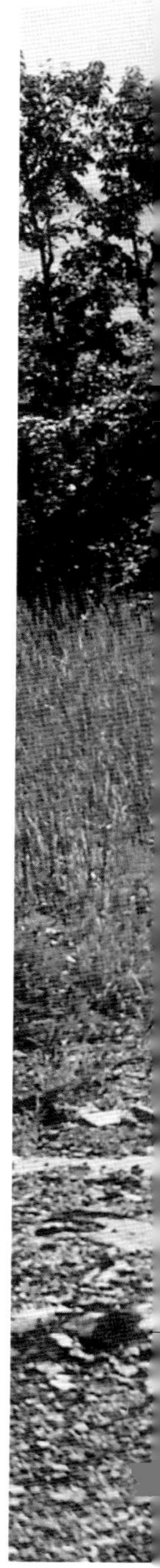

This photograph, taken in the summer of 1940, is without a doubt the finest image ever created of the Pennsylvania Turnpike. It was captured by the photographer Herbert Gehr and appeared in the July 29 issue of *Life* magazine. Included in an article entitled "Super-Highway," it previewed the soon-to-open road. The photograph was taken from atop Clear Ridge Cut. The identity of the man is unknown, but the details of the scene are easily identifiable. Immediately below him is one of the turnpike's classic rigid-frame concrete-arch bridges carrying Ritchey Road over the new highway. Beyond the bridge, the turnpike wends its way through a series of cuts and fills just east of the town of Everett. In the distance looms Tussey Mountain, bisected by Aliquippa Gap. This was the only break in the ridge for many miles north or south and the passageway through the mountains that would allow the turnpike to proceed west toward Pittsburgh. What cannot be known about the photograph is what the man pictured was thinking as he gazed at the almost-finished highway. One can only speculate that he was looking at the road with a sense of awe as he viewed what was clearly an unparalleled feat of civil engineering. More than any other photograph of the highway, this one embodies the glory about to be bestowed upon the Pennsylvania Turnpike. (Herbert Gehr, the Life Images Collection–Getty Images.)

The date is September 5, 1940. The location is the Straightaway east of Blue Mountain. After nearly two years of construction, the highway is ready for opening day.

OPPOSITE: This is the highway as it appeared shortly before it opened to traffic on October 1, 1940. These were the famous curves just east of Fort Littleton, one of the most photogenic spots on the entire highway. The photograph epitomizes everything about the brand-new Pennsylvania Turnpike that would captivate those who would use it for years to come—a gleaming, almost white concrete highway traversing the farmland and mountains of southern Pennsylvania and unlike any highway that had ever existed before.

FOUR

THE GLORY YEARS

As the summer of 1940 wore on, the late June deadline for completion was missed, as were several extensions. Finally, work drew to a close near the end of September. The announcement went out that the turnpike would be thrown open to traffic at midnight, October 1, 1940. No ceremony was planned. Instead, motorists and the curious alike began to line up at tollbooths, referred to as "ticket offices" at the time, waiting to be amongst the first to drive on the new highway.

The road they would see that day was unlike any ever built up to that time. No express highway had ever been constructed that passed through such rugged territory or rigidly adhered to such consistent engineering and geometrical standards throughout its length. Even more amazing was the fact that 160 miles of four-lane highway was opened in one fell swoop.

Unforeseen by the men who planned it, the turnpike immediately became the object of public fascination and admiration. Motorists flocked from throughout the country to take a drive on the brand-new Pennsylvania Turnpike. Most wondrous of all were the seven tunnels that pierced the ridges of the "Endless Mountains." For those who used it solely as a means of transportation, the time required to traverse the mountains of Pennsylvania was cut in half. Gone was the need to negotiate the curves and hills of the Lincoln and William Penn Highways along with the constant shifting of gears and use of brakes.

In its first year of operation, there was no posted speed limit on the new superhighway. Motorists would race along the road while attempting to traverse its 160-mile length as quickly as possible. Once home, they would compare notes to see who made the journey the quickest.

The turnpike became more than a means of getting somewhere. It became an attraction and a tourist destination in and of itself. Families flocked to the new facility to have their photographs taken at the tollbooths, along the roadside, and of course at the seven amazing tunnels.

The service plaza structures were built of quarried fieldstone to represent typical Colonial Pennsylvania architecture. None was as famous as South Midway, flagship of all the service plazas. A special treat was to stop at "the Midway" for a meal in the formal dining room. In that era, travelers took the time for a sit-down dinner in an elegant setting that included a huge fireplace. Food service was provided by the famed restaurateur Howard Johnson. While the other service plazas were much smaller, their names, such as Cove Valley and Blue Mountain, would become part of the turnpike's mystique.

Those travelers seeking a less formal meal would often dine on a picnic lunch packed before their journey began. As incredible as it seems today, while most usually picnicked alongside the road, some brave souls actually ate their meal in the grassy median strip!

The service plazas sold all manner of souvenirs, such as glasses, pennants, and dinner plates, celebrating the new highway. Most famous were the series of black-and-white and later color postcards that would be sent by turnpike patrons to their friends and families telling of their journey on the new highway. Perhaps the most memorable of them all were those that proclaimed the turnpike "The World's Greatest Highway," a moniker that would be associated with the highway for years to come.

There was no doubt about it. The Pennsylvania Turnpike was a smashing success. "The World's Greatest Highway," used repeatedly on postcards and Pennsylvania Turnpike Commission publications, was not merely a self-promotional boast. It was the truth.

The new road slashed across the mountains of Pennsylvania, reducing a trip that formerly took the better part of a day down to less than three hours. In this image, the turnpike can be seen disappearing into Blue Mountain Tunnel, hidden by the trees near the top center of the picture. This is where Pennsylvania's Great Valley ended and the Appalachian Mountains began. Note how the road first turns to the left, then to the right, thereby striking the ridge at a right angle, exactly as Col. Charles Schlatter had envisioned for the South Penn a half-century earlier.

This image of the ascent up the side of the ridge just east of the Bedford interchange was one of the most striking ones taken of the new highway. Interestingly, the information provided on the back of the photograph is completely erroneous. Dated November 5, 1940, it reads, "View of the Turnpike in the 'Bedford Narrows', looking east. . . . The 'Lincoln Highway', US Rt. #30 is shown on right." In fact, the view is taken approximately two miles west of the Bedford Narrows, the highway to the right is actually US Route 220, and the image was probably recorded in September, just before the turnpike opened. The presence of leaves on the trees, the signposts without a sign on the downgrade, and the rolled bales of hay on the shoulder are all giveaways.

Here is a publicity shot used by Westinghouse Electric Company to promote the usage of its sodium vapor lights to illuminate the interchanges. The lights produced a brilliant amber-colored light. The photograph was taken just west of the scene on the previous page. Much of the Bedford interchange can clearly be seen. This is one of a series of promotional photographs created by Westinghouse, and while undated, is believed to have been taken just days before the turnpike opened.

Given the presence of just a single vehicle and the lack of pavement markings, this was probably a staged photograph taken shortly before the turnpike opened. The image was created on the Straightaway, the arrow-straight section of the turnpike 12 miles long. It began at the Blue Mountain service plaza and stretched east to the Newville maintenance area. The crest of Blue Mountain forms the horizon line and was the first ridge of the Appalachians encountered by westbound motorists.

This is another clearly staged photograph meant to promote the new facility. The use of perfectly positioned vehicles, both from the same trucking company, is a dead giveaway. The date and location are unknown. Unlike the prior image, pavement markings have now been painted, but it is unclear if the highway was yet open to traffic.

With the opening of the turnpike on October 1, 1940, the Pennsylvania Turnpike Commission no longer had to rely on staged photographs. The above image appears to have been taken in 1941. This is evidenced by the "Speed Limit 70" sign. These were erected after a speed limit was put in place in April of that year, and with the onset of the United States involvement in World War II, the speed limit was temporarily lowered to 35 miles per hour. The photograph was taken between Somerset and Laurel Hill Tunnel and is looking to the west. The view below was taken from the bottom of a long grade a few miles east of the Donegal interchange. This is the same area pictured in the construction photograph on page 71. In the fields and woods to the right could be found the westernmost known grades of the South Penn. (Above, Library of Congress.)

The above image was taken near Quemahoning Tunnel, a few miles west of Somerset. It was one of two South Penn tunnels bypassed by the turnpike, the other being Negro Mountain a few miles east of Somerset. This photograph is from the same series of images as the upper picture on the opposite page, taken in 1941. The below picture shows the eastern approach to Allegheny Mountain Tunnel. It appears to have been taken from the portal itself. The westbound roadway, which is about to enter the tunnel, has narrowed to a single lane and already has a heavy grease streak due to the extra work needed by vehicle engines to climb the grade from New Baltimore. The abandoned grade of the South Penn can be seen diverging from the turnpike in the center of the photograph. It was not used by the turnpike because its less severe grade of just under two percent was considerably longer and more circuitous than the route used by the highway. (Above, Library of Congress.)

The new highway was also documented by means of aerial photography. This is a spectacular view of Aliquippa Gap, the passageway through Tussey Mountain just west of Everett. The Raystown Branch of the Juniata River parallels the turnpike to the left. Everett is at the upper left corner. The curving railroad bridge near the left center was an abandoned spur of the Huntingdon & Broad Top Mountain Railroad (H&BTM). It served a merchant blast furnace of the Joseph E. Thropp Company that once made pig iron at the site of the present-day Everett maintenance facility. That right-of-way was severed with the construction of the turnpike. The lower bridge is a branch of the Pennsylvania Railroad, which connected with the H&BTM. US Route 30 can be seen passing under the left end of that bridge near the bottom center of the image.

The Bedford Narrows was about four miles west of Aliquippa Gap and was the only break in Evitts Mountain for many miles to the north or south. As with Aliquippa Gap, it allowed passage of the turnpike, US Route 30, the Juniata River, and a branch of the Pennsylvania Railroad. The turnpike runs diagonally from the upper left to the lower right, and US 30 crosses the river on an unusual curved concrete-arch bridge. Though undated, the presence of patches on the transverse joints and the heavy grease streaking of the right lanes of the turnpike both suggest that this image was recorded a number of years after opening day.

The turnpike's seven tunnels were of course an obvious subject for the photographers retained by the commission. This image was created during the highway's first winter in service and is dated February 4, 1941. Shown is the eastern portal of Allegheny Mountain Tunnel, and the vehicle is a 1941 Studebaker Champion. It is parked at roughly the same spot as the auto with its hood up in the photograph at the bottom of page 95. To the right of the tunnel portal can be seen the unfinished South Penn bore, which was not utilized by the turnpike due to unstable rock.

One of the classic tunnel images repeatedly recorded of the turnpike was the view between Kittatinny and Blue Mountain Tunnels. Separated by just a few hundred feet, they never failed to surprise and delight first-time turnpike travelers who would immediately exit one tunnel only to quickly enter another. One was often photographed from within the portal of the adjacent tunnel, as in this image looking west from Blue Mountain Tunnel. Often a patrol officer was pictured within the near tunnel, but in this case, a wrecker is the focus of attention. The image is dated May 13, 1941, and was recorded by Jean Schwartz.

Westinghouse Electric Company utilized its promotional images of the tunnel lighting in its advertising. This advertisement appeared in the November 1940 issue of *The American City*. The upper image attempts to convey the brilliance of the new mercury vapor lamps used within the tunnels. The inset at lower right illustrates the use of sodium vapor lights at the tunnel approaches. These are part of the same series of images as shown on page 91.

This is an unusual view looking out of one of the tunnels at night and is another in the series of Westinghouse promotional photographs. The metal discs mounted along the center line would jar motorists drifting out of their lane, gain their attention, and prompt them to get back into their lane to avoid a head-on collision. With the passage of time, they would gradually loosen. One was eventually made airborne by a passing vehicle and struck another vehicle, resulting in an accident. As a result, they were removed. The date and location are unknown, but it appears to be the same portal as shown on the opposite page.

The tollbooths were another frequent subject of the photographer's lens. This is an image of the facility at the western terminus of Irwin not long after the highway opened. This booth served exiting motorists, and tolls were collected before the vehicle proceeded to US Route 30. Note the guardrail erected in front of the toll both to act as a crash barrier.

This is an image of the Carlisle tollbooth at the other end of the highway. While not dated, given the condition of the concrete curb and the vehicles shown in the image, this photograph was clearly taken long after opening day. An unused toll ticket is shown at the bottom of the page. A notation on the reverse side states "Revised, July 24, 1945." The toll for automobiles was a penny a mile, and it was not raised for many years. This ticket is for a much heavier Class 8 vehicle, the classification being performed visually by the toll collector as the vehicle passed through the tollbooth. As such, the tolls are considerably higher than those charged for an automobile.

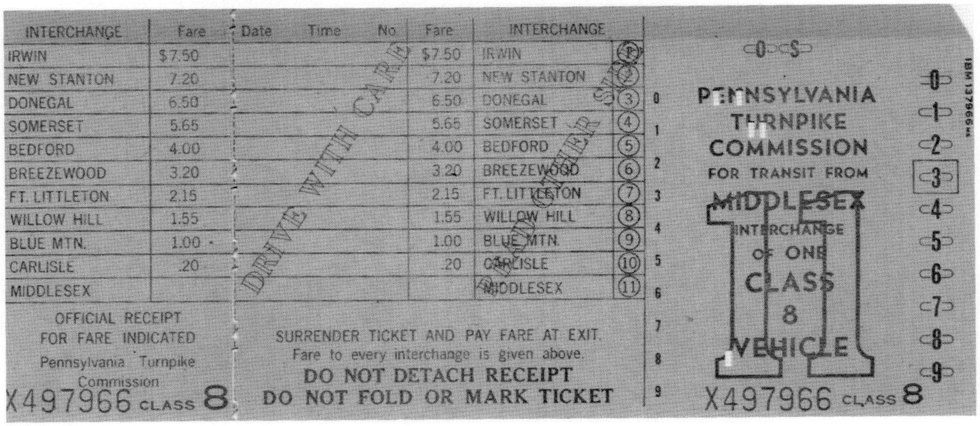

INTERCHANGE	Fare	Date	Time	No.	Fare	INTERCHANGE
IRWIN	$7.50				$7.50	IRWIN (1)
NEW STANTON	7.20				7.20	NEW STANTON (2)
DONEGAL	6.50				6.50	DONEGAL (3)
SOMERSET	5.65				5.65	SOMERSET (4)
BEDFORD	4.00				4.00	BEDFORD (5)
BREEZEWOOD	3.20				3.20	BREEZEWOOD (6)
FT. LITTLETON	2.15				2.15	FT. LITTLETON (7)
WILLOW HILL	1.55				1.55	WILLOW HILL (8)
BLUE MTN.	1.00				1.00	BLUE MTN. (9)
CARLISLE	.20				.20	CARLISLE (10)
MIDDLESEX						MIDDLESEX (11)

DRIVE WITH CARE

OFFICIAL RECEIPT FOR FARE INDICATED
Pennsylvania Turnpike Commission
X497966 CLASS 8

SURRENDER TICKET AND PAY FARE AT EXIT.
Fare to every interchange is given above.
DO NOT DETACH RECEIPT
DO NOT FOLD OR MARK TICKET

PENNSYLVANIA TURNPIKE COMMISSION
FOR TRANSIT FROM
MIDDLESEX
INTERCHANGE
OF ONE
CLASS
8
VEHICLE
11
X497966 CLASS 8

The volume of traffic at the intermediate interchanges was considerably less than at the terminals of Irwin and Carlisle. Accordingly, the toll facilities were much smaller, having but a single lane in each direction. Pictured here is the tollbooth at the Bedford interchange.

The turnpike passed through desolate areas of Pennsylvania, and when first opened, few if any services were available at the interchanges. The above image is the Breezewood interchange, looking west along US Route 30, the Lincoln Highway. The below image shows a billboard erected near the Willow Hill exit that promotes a motel. With the passage of time, things would change at Breezewood, which became famous as the "Town of Motels," not to mention numerous gas stations and restaurants. By comparison, more than 75 years after the opening of the turnpike, Willow Hill, as well as the nearby Blue Mountain and Fort Littleton interchanges, remain very rural, with few roadside services.

Given the paucity of roadside services along its route, the turnpike established service plazas at intervals of roughly 30 miles along the new highway. When opened, most were diminutive structures, offering fuel, a lunch counter, and restrooms. They quickly proved to be inadequate and were rapidly expanded, as can be seen in this view of the Blue Mountain facility. Note the photographer's car, which also appears in the image of the Bedford tollbooth on page 104.

Unlike the other service plaza facilities, South Midway offered sit-down dining facilities with a full dining room, showers, a truckers' dormitory, and other amenities. It was clearly the flagship of all the service plazas and quickly became a tourist destination. The name "Midway" derived from the fact that it was located at about the midpoint of the 160-mile turnpike. Like its smaller brethren, it too was expanded not long after opening. Witness the frame extension with the arched windows at the right side of the structure.

Here are two postcard views from 1940 that show the service plazas as they looked when first opened. The above image is of the Path Valley plaza. The structure is very small and lacks the frame addition seen on the Blue Mountain structure on page 106. There are just two islands with gasoline pumps and only a handful of parking spaces. The image below shows the structures at both North (foreground) and South Midway. North Midway was particularly small, as a pedestrian tunnel below the turnpike linked the two buildings and allowed westbound travelers to access the dining facilities at South Midway. The latter had considerably more gas pumps than the other plazas, as well as a separate service station facility. Parking is abundant, and South Midway was the only building to be fronted by a large front lawn and an elegant circular driveway. The back of the postcard indicates that the restaurant could seat 120 patrons when first opened.

This is an outstanding image of the Cove Valley service plaza in service in early 1952. Traffic volumes had increased considerably since opening day 12 years earlier, as is reflected in the large number of cars and increased number of gas pumps in place to serve them. Even without the automobiles and expanded parking and fueling area, the 1950s-type guardrail at the extreme right of the picture is a tip-off as to the era when the image was created.

Here is another 1950s image of one of the service plazas. Howard Johnson's had been awarded the franchise for the dining facilities, while Esso Marketers (Standard Oil Company of Pennsylvania) held the franchise for the service stations.

The license plate at the bottom of this photograph gives away the year as 1942. During the war years, women served in the roles usually associated with men in many areas of the nation's workforce. At this time, the speed limit was lowered from 70 miles per hour to 35 to conserve gasoline.

The service stations located at each of the service plazas could perform routine maintenance and basic repairs. Flat tires were of course a common issue, and the facilities were stocked with a supply of tires. Here, a truck full of them is being unloaded along with other supplies at Cove Valley.

Aside from performing minor repairs and maintenance, the turnpike service stations sold a variety of sundries, including sunglasses, seat cushions, and watch straps, as can be seen in the display case. This is a photograph of the service station at Midway.

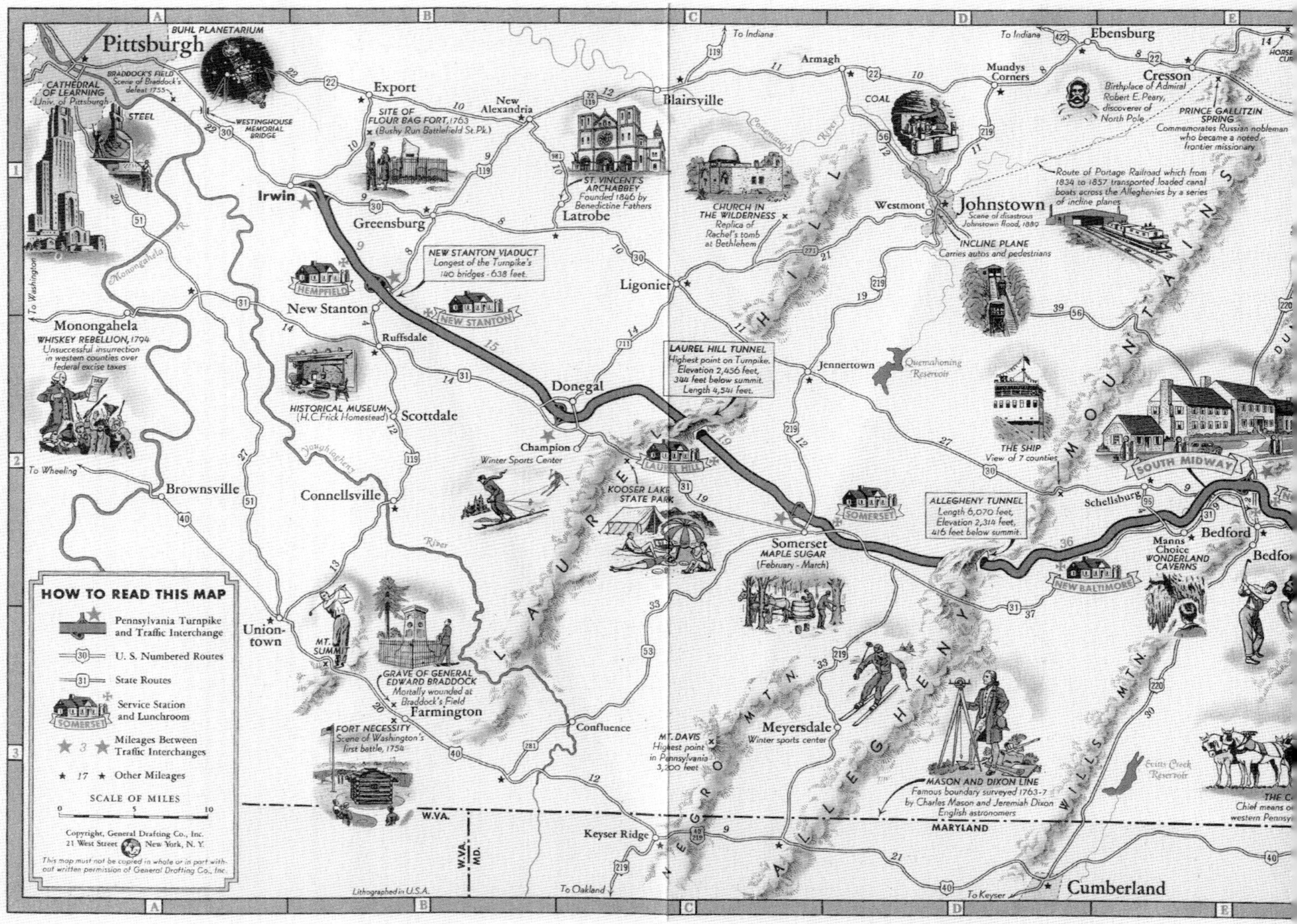

Road maps were routinely distributed by service stations in the 1940s. This one was probably the best amongst them in illustrating the new highway and was part of a souvenir map and brochure that sold for 25¢. The map provided the location of the interchanges, service plazas, and tunnels. Even the configuration of the ramps comprising the interchanges could be seen. Small illustrations of scenic and historical attractions made easily accessible by the new highway were included as well. In addition to the map, the brochure provided a concise history of the turnpike, including mention of the abandoned South Penn. Finally, there were facts and figures about the turnpike, such as the number of bridges and amounts of materials used in its construction, as well as a table allowing patrons to calculate their toll.

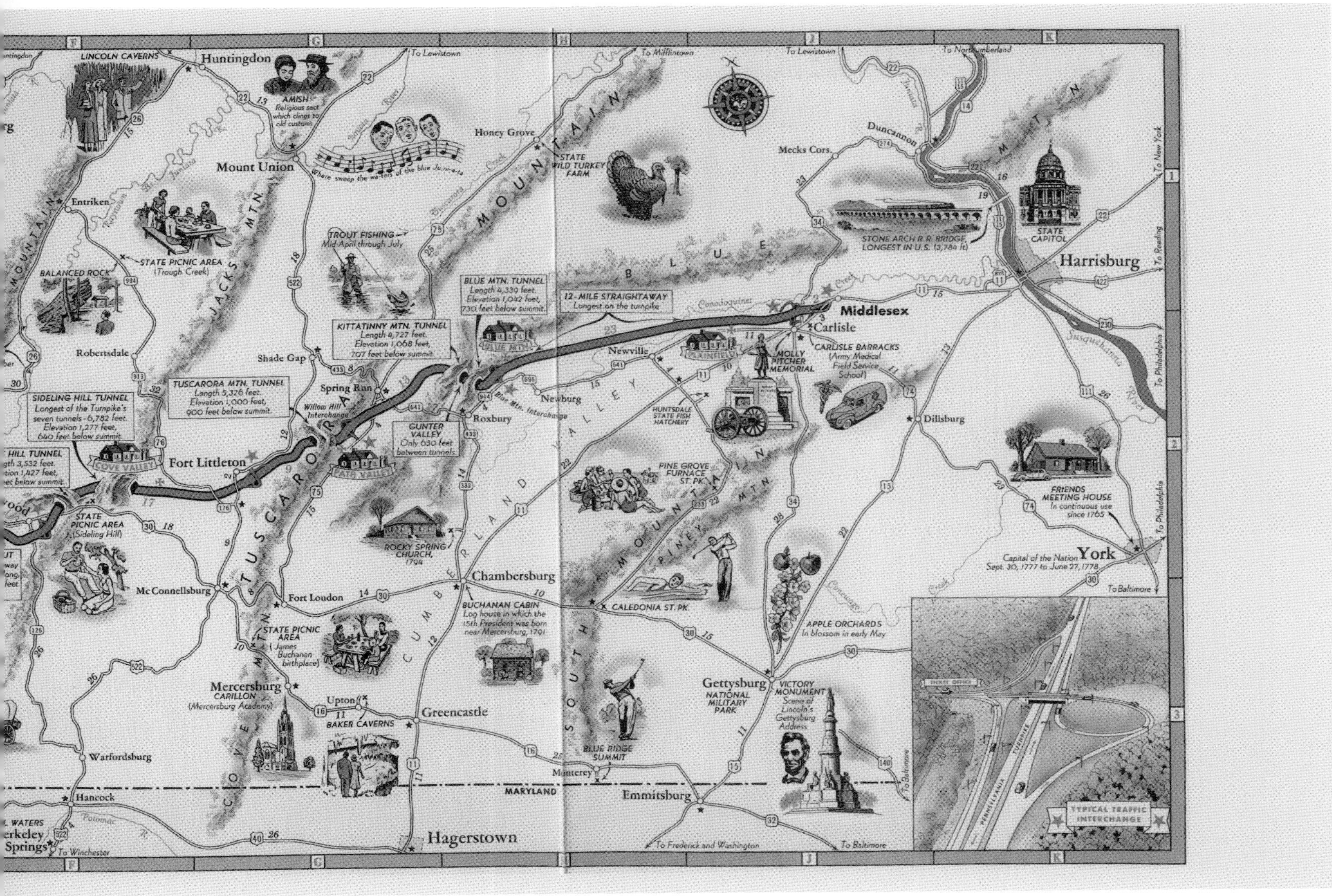

LINCOLN CAVERNS
Huntingdon
AMISH
Religious sect which clings to old customs
To Lewistown
Honey Grove
STATE WILD TURKEY FARM
To Mifflintown
To Lewistown
To Northumberland
Duncannon
Mecks Cors.
Mount Union
Where sweep the waters of the blue Juniata
Entriken
STATE PICNIC AREA
(Trough Creek)
BALANCED ROCK
TROUT FISHING
Mid-April through July
JACKS MTN.
BLUE MOUNTAIN
BLUE MTN.
STONE ARCH R.R. BRIDGE
LONGEST IN U.S. (3,780 ft)
STATE CAPITOL
Harrisburg
To Reading
To New York
BLUE MTN. TUNNEL
Length 4,339 feet.
Elevation 1,042 feet,
730 feet below summit.
12-MILE STRAIGHTAWAY
Longest on the turnpike
Conodoguinet Creek
Middlesex
Carlisle
KITTATINNY MTN. TUNNEL
Length 4,727 feet.
Elevation 1,068 feet,
707 feet below summit.
Robertsdale
Shade Gap
Newville
PLAINFIELD
MOLLY PITCHER MEMORIAL
CARLISLE BARRACKS
(Army Medical Field Service School)
Susquehanna River
To Philadelphia
TUSCARORA MTN. TUNNEL
Length 5,326 feet.
Elevation 1,000 feet,
900 feet below summit.
SIDELING HILL TUNNEL
Longest of the Turnpike's seven tunnels - 6,782 feet.
Elevation 1,277 feet,
640 feet below summit.
Spring Run
Willow Hill Interchange
Blue Mtn. Interchange
Newburg
Roxbury
GUNTER VALLEY
Only 650 feet between tunnels.
HUNTSDALE STATE FISH HATCHERY
Dillsburg
Fort Littleton
COVE VALLEY
PATH VALLEY
TUSCARORA
PINE GROVE FURNACE ST. PK.
FRIENDS MEETING HOUSE
In continuous use since 1765
STATE PICNIC AREA
(Sideling Hill)
ROCKY SPRING CHURCH, 1794
CUMBERLAND VALLEY
SOUTH MOUNTAIN
PINEY MTN.
Capital of the Nation
Sept. 30, 1777 to June 27, 1778
York
To Baltimore
McConnellsburg
Fort Loudon
Chambersburg
CALEDONIA ST. PK.
BUCHANAN CABIN
Log house in which the 15th President was born near Mercersburg, 1791
STATE PICNIC AREA
(James Buchanan birthplace)
APPLE ORCHARDS
In blossom in early May
Mercersburg
CARILLON
(Mercersburg Academy)
Upton
BAKER CAVERNS
Greencastle
Gettysburg
NATIONAL MILITARY PARK
VICTORY MONUMENT
Scene of Lincoln's Gettysburg Address
COVE MTN.
BLUE RIDGE SUMMIT
Monterey
Warfordsburg
Hancock
MARYLAND
Emmitsburg
To Baltimore
Potomac R.
Hagerstown
To Winchester
To Frederick and Washington
To Baltimore
TICKET OFFICE
PENNSYLVANIA TURNPIKE
TYPICAL TRAFFIC INTERCHANGE

The service plazas also sold turnpike souvenirs, given the highway's newfound popularity with the public. They included plates, glasses, salt shakers, and pennants. But none were as famous as the series of postcards. First in black and white, and later featuring colorized images, hundreds of different views would be published that illustrated every facet of the turnpike. The above image immortalizes the turnpike through its powerful use of outlined block letters, each containing a different image of the turnpike. The view between Kittatinny and Blue Mountain Tunnels can be seen in the background. The below image is almost identical to that immortalized by Herbert Gehr, albeit now in full color.

Later, postcards and souvenir booklets began to use actual photographs rather than artistic colorized images. Many of them included monikers glorifying the turnpike. While a number of slogans were used, none appeared so frequently as "The World's Greatest Highway," seen on the cover of this brochure. This publication included the turnpike's Northeastern Extension, dating it to at least 1957, evidence that even after almost two decades, the public was still fascinated by the Pennsylvania Turnpike.

The use of staged photographs included not only the tunnels, bridges, and open road but even the stylized exit signs. Here is one of those signs, which featured demountable reflectorized block lettering. The circular exit number at top added a bit of artistry. Note the woman's elegant fur coat. Didn't everybody travel the Pennsylvania Turnpike dressed this way? The car is the same one seen on page 98.

This is another in the series of photographs created by Westinghouse to promote the lighting equipment it supplied for the turnpike. The tight curve to the left just beyond the tunnel portal reveals that the image was recorded at the eastern end of Allegheny Mountain Tunnel. The caption supplied with the photograph implies that the couple were travelers who parked their car outside the tunnel, then walked up to the portal to take a closer look. In reality, such practices would probably have been frowned upon, even in that era.

Though the turnpike commission may have staged photographs in order to generate publicity, the new highway fascinated the public, which flocked to have their pictures taken along the road without being prompted by the commission. The tunnels of course were the most intriguing feature of the new highway. Both of these photographs were obtained from privately held collections, and the names of the individuals are unknown. The photograph below is dated June 1946. The date of the above photograph is unknown, as are the specific locations of both images.

While the tunnels may have been the biggest attraction on the turnpike, travelers would stop almost anywhere along the road to have their picture taken. Also obtained from a private collection, the only information available about the above image is that it was taken at Willow Hill in 1941 as is handwritten across the top. Willow Hill was among the most desolate of all of the exits along the turnpike and as such saw little traffic, so the reason for the cars lined up to exit the highway is uncertain. The below image was taken at South Midway in 1947. Two unidentified women walk up the circular drive to the front entrance of the service plaza building. Stopping at the South Midway Howard Johnson's for a meal was always a treat. Taking the time for a sit-down meal was the norm in that era.

As the 1950s drew to a close, subtle changes were occurring on the Pennsylvania Turnpike that would signal a dramatic shift in the public's perception of the highway. The unkempt appearance of the tunnel portal, the messy gravel shoulder, and the absence of pavement markings were all clues that something was amiss. Taken together, all of this portended dark days ahead for "The World's Greatest Highway."

OPPOSITE: This group began their tour of the turnpike at the western terminus near Irwin. Apparently passing through the "ticket office," as they were referred to at this time, the photographer turned around and shot this image looking west toward US Route 30.

FIVE

TOURING THE TURNPIKE

Although the long-term future of the turnpike may have been unclear, in late 1940, everything looked bright for the new highway. This was exemplified by one of the best collections of turnpike photographs ever discovered. It is believed to have been created by a group of automobile industry executives. The collection was privately held, and the images were all mounted in a small black photo album. The name of the owner, Sidney D. Waldon of Detroit, appeared inside the front cover.

The precise details of the trip are unknown, and no dates were provided. In looking at the trees along the turnpike, some have just a few leaves, suggesting that the images were recorded in late October or early November 1940. Apparently the group travelled from Detroit to Pittsburgh prior to setting out on their journey to tour the brand-new Pennsylvania Turnpike. Evidence of this is provided in the first few images in the album, which contains photographs not just of downtown Pittsburgh, but several highways and bridges within the city as well. The subsequent photograph in the album is of US Route 30 a few miles west of the Irwin interchange, confirming that this is the route they used to access the new highway.

The party clearly had a great deal of knowledge about the turnpike prior to their journey. While they photographed the obvious scenes, such as the tunnels, tollbooths, and service plazas, they had knowledge of other locations that the casual turnpike traveler would never have been aware

of. The viaduct at New Stanton is a case in point. Aside from the parapets, the structure was hardly visible from the road and would be easy to miss. The story was different from the roadside. From the group's vantage point at the western abutment, the impressive center span, an open-spandrel concrete arch, and multiple side spans were all plainly visible.

More noteworthy was their stop to view the eastern portal of Quemahoning Tunnel. This landmark was not visible to the passing motorist. Clearly they were made aware of its location, as well as its historical significance. Their lunch at South Midway was served to them in a private upstairs dining room and is a tip-off that the trip was not only well planned, but quite possibly arranged through the turnpike commission. The detailed notations in the album regarding the construction statistics about Clear Ridge Cut are particularly impressive.

In many of the photographs, it is apparent that the group not only stopped, but crossed the highway to obtain their images, such as at Quemahoning and Allegheny Tunnels. Given the presence of the concrete median barrier in place today, that would no longer be possible. And even without its presence, crossing the highway today would be extremely dangerous and would likely earn them a citation from the Pennsylvania State Police!

Besides the typically photographed tunnels and tollbooths, the photographer captured images of several scenes rarely, if ever, seen in other pictures of the turnpike. One of the most impressive is that taken from the bottom of the cut face of Tussey Mountain. The image gives a sense of the extent of the work and the height of the cut and is a wonderful photograph of the road as it twists its way through Aliquippa Gap. Other rarely photographed scenes include the Hazelette Street bridge near Everett, Laurel Hill service plaza, and the long tangent by Kegg, spanned by numerous concrete T-beam bridges.

But it is not just their subject matter that is special. The collection is unique because all of the images appear to have been taken on a single day, are accurately labeled, are generally mounted in the correct sequential order, and all are of excellent quality. For that reason, of the 29 images of the turnpike in the album, 24 of them have been reproduced here. Any captioning and sequence errors have been corrected in order to provide a sense of what the group experienced as they toured the new highway.

The first stop on the tour was the New Stanton Viaduct. This structure was the largest bridge on the turnpike and spanned US Route 119, a branch of the Pennsylvania Railroad, and a stream. It was located immediately east of the New Stanton interchange and consisted of a reinforced concrete arch and several side spans.

The group of executives then resumed their eastbound journey on the turnpike. As with this image, many were taken by the front passenger directly through the windshield. The location is vaguely identified as being somewhere "west of Donegal." In fact, it is much closer to New Stanton, its precise location being just west of the present-day Pennsylvania Route 981 underpass. Chestnut Ridge, the westernmost ridge of the Alleghenies, can be seen in the distance.

The next image was taken just west of the Donegal interchange, which is located at the other end of the cut seen in the distance. Pennsylvania Route 31 can be seen off to the right. It generally paralleled the turnpike between New Stanton and a point a few miles west of Bedford.

Laurel Hill was the first of the seven tunnels they would encounter during their journey. It was the highest point along the turnpike, so it was not unusual to see snow in the area this early in the season. It was the first tunnel to experience traffic backups in the 1950s. As such, it was bypassed in 1964.

The group stopped at the Laurel Hill service plaza, which was located about two miles east of the tunnel. Even at that early date, the facility was clearly unable to handle the number of vehicles that stopped there. It was later enlarged, and eventually it and the New Baltimore plaza were replaced by the much larger intermediate South Somerset plaza. Of the thousands of turnpike images reviewed by the authors, this is the only one they are aware of that captured the Laurel Hill service plaza.

The photographer took this image of the ramp leading into the Laurel Hill service plaza. As was the case with all of the turnpike ramps, it was built of asphalt rather than concrete. Despite the large number of vehicles parked at the facility, note the relative paucity of traffic on the turnpike itself. The view is looking to the west.

The group had clearly researched the history of the new highway. In this image, one of them peers into the portal of the bypassed Quemahoning Tunnel, which was located less than 50 feet north of the highway. Since the opening sat below the level of the road and was not at all obvious to travelers, only those with an intimate knowledge of the highway would have been able to locate the tunnel portal.

Allegheny Mountain Tunnel was the second tunnel the group would encounter. It was the second longest of the turnpike tunnels and was the only tunnel to utilize a completely new bore due to unstable rock in the original South Penn tunnel. The original portal was hidden behind the left side of the tunnel facade.

The group stopped at Allegheny Mountain Tunnel to have their photograph taken. Posing for photographs at the tunnels was not unusual in the early years of the turnpike. As traffic grew over time, crossing the highway directly in front of a tunnel portal would become a dangerous proposition.

During their visit, they captured this image of the tunnel interior. The recessed mercury vapor lights and the bare concrete walls of the tunnel are clearly seen. Lacking a white tile lining, the walls could not be washed and would gradually accumulate dirt and soot and darken over time. Compare this image to that on page 100 created by Westinghouse Electric Company. In reality, the tunnel interiors were not nearly as bright as suggested by promotional photographs.

Immediately upon exiting Allegheny Mountain Tunnel, the group began its descent down the Allegheny escarpment. It was almost seven miles in length, and the road twisted and turned due to the rugged terrain. This area of the turnpike was always the most difficult part of the drive between Irwin and Carlisle, particularly during the winter.

Near the bottom of the grade, the group encountered an area of the mountain prone to rock slides, as seen at right. This section of the turnpike was a problem for the construction crews who built the turnpike, as well as the maintenance workers who would take care of the highway after it opened. Not until 2015 did work begin to straighten the curve and permanently address the unstable slope.

Once the tour group reached the bottom of the grade, they continued east on a long stretch of the turnpike that was almost level and free of curves. There was a particularly high concentration of the concrete T-beam bridges in this area. The skies looked menacing as the convoy headed east.

Eventually, the group reached the South Midway service plaza. A stop for lunch here was of course obligatory as part of their tour of the turnpike. This outstanding close-up view shows the Colonial Pennsylvania stone architecture in detail. The looped entrance drive is to the left.

The executives were treated to lunch in a private dining room on the upper floor of the service plaza building. This was an area of the building seldom seen by turnpike travelers, especially in later years.

Resuming their journey, the next stop was the huge cut just west of Everett, as pictured in the panoramic view on pages 36 and 37. The photographer's notes state that the face of the cut was 235 feet high. Ashcom Road can be seen above the automobiles and was built on a terrace carved into the cliff above the turnpike. The abandoned railroad trestle leading into the Joseph E. Thropp iron-making furnace at Everett can be seen to the left.

Less than a mile to the east, the caravan passed the Everett maintenance facility, just out of view to the right. In the distance can be seen the Hazelette Street bridge, which is still in service today. The group's automobile is at about the same point where the railroad spur into the merchant iron furnace was located.

Proceeding another mile to the east, the group finds itself just south of Everett and approaching the Dogwood Lane bridge. Clear Ridge Cut can be seen in the distance, just above the center of the bridge.

At last, the convoy has reached Clear Ridge Cut, with the Ritchey Road bridge crossing the highway on the west end of the cut. The unidentified man in the Herbert Gehr photograph on page 84 was standing at the top of the cut at the extreme right edge of the image.

This is a close-up of Clear Ridge Cut, framed by the Ritchey Road bridge. Notations provided in the photo album state that the cut was 153 feet deep, 385 feet in width at the top, and 2,670 feet long; 1.35 million cubic yards of material were excavated, and 700,000 pounds of explosives were used in its excavation. Finally, it notes that the benches (the two shelves on the face of the cut designed to catch falling rock) were 20 feet wide.

The notes in the photo album erroneously labeled this image as being the "East End of Negro Mountain Cut, Somerset County." In reality, this photograph was taken from within Clear Ridge Cut and looks to the west. The Ritchey Road overpass and Tussey Mountain can both be seen in the distance. This is essentially the same view as that in the Herbert Gehr image but taken from 153 feet below.

Proceeding to the east, the group approached Breezewood. Just ahead is the Pointer Road bridge. Part of the barn seen to the right still exists today. The location would become best known for a series of billboards posted just to the right of the bridge and partially obscuring the farm structures. All proclaimed to eastbound travelers that they were approaching "Breezewood, Town of Motels."

The final image in the album was this photograph of the western portal of Sideling Hill Tunnel, east of Breezewood. The group still had many miles to go before reaching the eastern terminus near Carlisle, so it is unclear why the series of images stopped here. Did they turn around, run out of film, or is there a lost second album? Unfortunately, it probably will never be known for sure.

OPPOSITE: This image, taken later in the 1940s just east of Fort Littleton, provides the first subtle clues of the problems that were to beset the Pennsylvania Turnpike. Close inspection of the eastbound lanes (at right) reveals an unusually high number of transverse cracks for a highway of this age. Compare this to the image of the brand-new highway on page 87. This was the first evidence of an under-engineered highway incapable of handling the traffic loads it would be called upon to carry.

Six

Fall from Grace

So successful was the Pennsylvania Turnpike that in its first full year of operation, it carried almost twice the number of vehicles projected. Though that growth was temporarily halted by the outbreak of World War II, it resumed immediately after the war. Eventually, the turnpike became the victim of its own success. Beginning in the 1950s, heavy summer traffic led to traffic backups at Laurel Hill Tunnel as the highway narrowed to a single lane as it approached the tunnels. With time, the problem began to affect all of the tunnels. All of a sudden, the highway that had been a source of wonderment and amazement became an irritation to the motoring public.

There were other problems as well. Since the concrete roadway was poured directly on compacted earth without benefit of a gravel base, the concrete began to fail after just a few years. The rough ride no longer fit with the self-appointed title of "The World's Greatest Highway." The use of non-air-entrained concrete caused premature spalling of the concrete rigid-frame arch and T-beam bridges. In short, the highway was under-engineered and not capable of supporting the volume of traffic that it had attracted. This was not necessarily the result of poor design but simply reflective of the design standards of the day.

The highway's design also became prematurely obsolete. After the single-lane tunnels, the biggest

issue was the narrow 10-foot median. As traffic volumes rose, so did the number of fatal head-on collisions as a result of vehicles crossing the median. The Pennsylvania Turnpike Commission would address this problem by installing a steel median barrier. It was initially installed on sharp curves and areas with high accident rates. Eventually, it would span the length of the turnpike. While it may have reduced the number of accidents, it was no fun driving with that barrier just a few feet from one's left fender.

The obsolescence was also reflected in the tunnels and bridges. The tunnel interiors were dingy and poorly lit, and opposing traffic sped by just a few feet away. Heaven help the summer vacationer who entered the tunnel with the windows lowered while noisy tractor-trailer trucks barreled by in the opposite direction. The turnpike's distinctive concrete arch bridges with their ornate masonry also began to look dated in a postwar world more accustomed to purely functional designs.

Finally, the highway's maintenance was less than ideal. Some issues, such as the rough roadway surface would be difficult for any maintenance department to deal with given the under-engineered pavement design. But other problems, such as sooty tunnel portals overgrown with vines, fading hazard placards painted on bridge abutments, and a median and shoulders that were covered with cinders well into the spring, were harder to overlook. And that pesky narrow median with a dented, rust-tinged median barrier did not help matters.

Meanwhile, just as delays started to occur at the turnpike's tunnels, another engineering marvel was put into service roughly 150 miles to the east. In November 1951, the ultra-modern New Jersey Turnpike was opened to traffic. Unlike the Pennsylvania Turnpike, there was nothing quaint about this road. Brutally cutting across the New Jersey countryside, the road featured a median generally at least 26 feet in width (and sometimes much wider), utilitarian bridges that look contemporary even in today's world, and a whole host of other features that have stood the test of time. Even the New Jersey Turnpike's first annual report issued in 1949 brought these issues to light. The report stated that the new highway would feature "a center raised mall . . . separating traffic moving in opposite directions by at least 26 feet." It went on to specifically call out the Pennsylvania Turnpike by saying that the lanes would be "12 feet, the lanes in each direction to be flanked by a 10-foot finished shoulder on the outside, and by a 5-foot finished shoulder on the inside. (By comparison, the Pennsylvania Turnpike lanes are 12 feet wide, with a 10-foot shoulder outside, no inside shoulder, and a median strip 10 feet wide.)"

Surprisingly, while the New Jersey Turnpike featured modern geometry and architectural features, the eastern extension of the Pennsylvania Turnpike to Philadelphia, which had opened just a year earlier, continued to use all of the dated designs of the original section of the highway. The reality was that the New Jersey Turnpike represented the cutting edge of highway design. By contrast, the most charitable description one could use to describe the Pennsylvania Turnpike was "quaint."

One other factor that contributed to the turnpike's fall from grace was totally out of its control. That was opening of Interstate 80 across Pennsylvania to the north of the turnpike in 1970. It featured a wide median, smooth pavement (at least for a few years after opening), and modern bridge architecture. This would prove to be the final death blow to the image of the Pennsylvania Turnpike. Now motorists had a brand-new expressway that could be used to traverse the commonwealth. And even if the turnpike had been completely modernized to the standards of a modern-day interstate, there was still one other issue that would continue work to its disadvantage. One had to pay to use it.

By the early 1950s, it was apparent that the turnpike's concrete pavement was not holding up well. Some of the reasons for this included the fact that the concrete was poured directly on compacted earth rather than a stone base, as well as excessive slab length of approximately 77 feet. As the pavement failures became more widespread, the turnpike began to replace the worst sections of pavement with new concrete. The photograph above shows an example of this work in progress on the eastern approach to Allegheny Mountain Tunnel. Eventually, the problem became so widespread that it was more economical to simply apply an asphalt overlay. Although concrete pavement should have a life expectancy of about 20 years, repaving operations began in 1954 when the highway was just 14 years old. The initial work was a 21-mile stretch between Laurel Hill and Allegheny Mountain Tunnels. Pictured below is repaving work being performed a mile east of the New Stanton service plaza. The entire original section of the turnpike was resurfaced by 1962.

The once-magical tunnels had also become a significant problem by the 1950s. With just a single lane in each direction, traffic backups began to develop during the summer months, and the problem became worse with each passing year. The tunnel linings gradually darkened as more and more exhaust soot accumulated, rendering the mercury vapor lighting incapable of adequately illuminating the tunnels. The vine-covered portal was evidence of indifferent maintenance, and of course, just as with the rest of the road, the pavement approaching the tunnel was falling apart.

The tollbooth at Carlisle aged poorly as well. This image was taken in the late 1940s, before the facility was even 10 years old. Rust streaks are already evident on the architectural features above each traffic lane. The accumulation of cinders and the tire tracks across the median create the impression of a poorly maintained facility. The lighting fixtures mounted on wooden poles contribute to the image of a prematurely obsolete highway. The combination of rough pavement, dingy tunnels, and marginal maintenance would all contribute to the erosion of the public's perception of the highway.

On November 5, 1951, a little more than 150 miles to the east of Carlisle, another groundbreaking toll road would open that would immediately render obsolete the design of the Pennsylvania Turnpike. That highway was the New Jersey Turnpike. One did not have to be a highway engineer to immediately see the difference. This road featured a median generally at least 26 feet in width and sometimes much wider, modern multi-span overpasses with a contemporary architectural design, many miles of six-lane roadway, and service plazas set far back from the highway.

Compare the image of the New Jersey Turnpike to the one above, a promotional photograph of the Philadelphia extension of the Pennsylvania Turnpike. Opened on November 20, 1950, the highway was a contemporary of the New Jersey facility yet carried on the prewar design utilizing a narrow 10-foot median and architecturally dated bridges. At least the concrete roadway was now placed on a compacted stone base and had shorter slabs of 46 feet. Unfortunately, neither of those improvements was obvious to the public.

This image showing the eastern approach to Allegheny Mountain Tunnel epitomizes everything that had gone wrong with the Pennsylvania Turnpike by the 1970s. Evidence of under-engineering is apparent in the tight-radius curve. The bridge design is a relic of the prewar era. The faded painted hazard placard on the bridge abutment, accumulated cinders in the median, and worn-away pavement markings are all evidence of poor maintenance practices. But nothing was as bad as ascending this grade on a dark, snowy night with a tractor trailer to one's right and that rust-tinged median barrier just a few feet away from one's left fender. Compare this photograph to the image on page 73.

Though the greatest years of the Pennsylvania Turnpike were long gone, for those with an appreciation of the engineering and architecture of the turnpike, the legacy of "The World's Greatest Highway" remained very much alive. For them, nothing could be more heart-wrenching than the fate that befell the turnpike's legendary rigid-frame concrete-arch bridges. Seventy-five years after the highway opened, only a handful remained, and most were in horrendous condition. Perhaps saddest of all was the Ritchey Road bridge at the western end of Clear Ridge Cut, immortalized in Herbert Gehr's timeless photo essay in *Life* magazine. Gone were the architecturally complex parapets, now replaced by a solid slab of concrete and a chain-link fence, as seen in the above image. The photograph below reveals the extent of the structural damage to the bridge. All of this was the result of the combined effects of deicing salts, the use of non-air-entrained concrete, and time. (Both, Neal A. Schorr.)

More than any other photograph of the Pennsylvania Turnpike, none so vividly depicts the fate that would meet the nation's first long-distance superhighway. Pictured in 1970 along the 12-mile Straightaway east of Blue Mountain Tunnel, the highway is in deplorable condition. While the end of the glory years began some time in the 1950s, it would be impossible to say precisely when they came to an end. But this much is for certain. By 1970, they were clearly over.

OPPOSITE: The original two-lane tunnels were clearly the biggest problem facing the turnpike in the 1960s. The Pennsylvania Turnpike Commission responded accordingly by adding second bores at Allegheny, Tuscarora, Kittatinny, and Blue Mountain and bypassing Laurel, Rays, and Sideling Hill. In addition, the original tunnels were completely rehabilitated. The work included new white tile walls and continuous fluorescent lighting, which eliminated their dark and dingy interiors. All of the work was finished on March 18, 1971, with the completion of the rehabilitation of Kittatinny (shown opposite) and Blue Mountain Tunnels. (Neal A. Schorr.)

SIX

REBIRTH

Over the next 30 years, it was not as if the Pennsylvania Turnpike Commission was not making improvements and attempting to correct the deficiencies with the road. The biggest immediate problem was doing something about the single-lane tunnels. While not inexpensive, it was a straightforward problem to solve. At four sites, Allegheny, Tuscarora, Kittatinny, and Blue Mountain, new parallel tunnels were bored and the original tunnel was complexly rehabilitated. The three other tunnels, Laurel, Rays, and Sideling Hill, were bypassed completely. The work was completed shortly after I-80 was opened. Other improvements were made as well. The crumbling center-pier T-beam bridges were all replaced, truck lanes were added on some of the steeper sections in western Pennsylvania, and some of the dangerous curves on the grade descending from Allegheny Mountain Tunnel were straightened. Eventually, some parts of the highway were totally reconstructed from the base up, including the installation of subbase and entirely new pavement.

Still, a lack of foresight was evident in many of these projects. Most of the replacement bridges made no allowance for the inclusion of additional lanes. Particularly hard to understand was the base-up reconstruction of the section of turnpike just west of Kittatinny Mountain Tunnel. While upon completion it was structurally a completely new highway, the same four-lane cross-section, including the 10-foot median, was retained. Although the highway may have been brand

new, to the passing motorist, it looked like the same old road.

Finally, after roughly 40 years of benign neglect, things began to change on the Pennsylvania Turnpike. Around the beginning of the 21st century, the turnpike commission adopted a new approach to the reconstruction of the highway. Rather than just rebuilding the highway with geometry similar to the original road or only slightly improved, significant improvements would now be made. The road would be widened to six lanes. Curves would be straightened. All replacement bridges would be built to accommodate additional lanes. And finally, something would be done about that annoying narrow median. The new cross-section called for a median 26 feet in width, allowing for 12-foot-wide left shoulders and a two-foot-wide concrete median barrier. At last, the turnpike would catch up with it postwar brethren interstates.

With the adoption of the new six-lane design, a new overpass design was also devised. Back was the center pier bridge, albeit now with steel or prestressed concrete girders. With a concrete median barrier in place along the entire turnpike, the center pier could now be safely embedded within the barrier without concern that it would be a hazard to errant motorists. But the most important aspect of the design was the attention to aesthetics. Replacement bridges constructed prior to the beginning of the 21th century were utilitarian structures devoid of any architectural details. Now many of the bridges were built with faux stone or brick masonry work on the wing walls and parapets, reminiscent of the architectural touches applied to the old rigid-frame concrete-arch bridges.

The commission also recognized that the original service plaza buildings had reached the end of their useful life. Their original design had been chosen to portray Colonial Pennsylvania stone architecture. Accordingly, the commission directed that the exterior of their replacements be of the same architectural style. The inside was an altogether different story. The interior was a large food court surrounded by quick-serve food vendors, a convenience store, and huge dual restrooms to permit cleaning without the need for closure, all consistent with the needs and desires of today's travelers.

With these efforts at real reconstruction under way, the Pennsylvania Turnpike is slowly shedding its image as an under-maintained and obsolete highway. The process is a slow one, undertaken a few miles at a time. The reconstruction of each segment typically costs more than construction of the entire original turnpike in dollars not adjusted for inflation.

There is one downside to this work. With its modernization, the highway is slowly losing much of its original character as it is figuratively converted from the Pennsylvania Turnpike to I-76. The Pennsylvania Turnpike Commission's attention to bridge aesthetics and retention of the architectural flavor of the service plaza buildings has helped to keep alive the memory of the turnpike as it was on its opening day. Furthermore, some things cannot be changed. There will always be tunnels piercing the "Endless Mountains," the huge cut at Clear Ridge, and those timeless exit names such as Willow Hill, Blue Mountain, and most famous of all, Breezewood. Together, all of this will help to preserve and restore the glory that was the Pennsylvania Turnpike.

As the turnpike entered its fifth decade of service in 1980, many of the bridges approached the end of their design life. The center-pier concrete T-beam bridges would be the most vulnerable. Their center piers were fully exposed to the corrosive effects of deicing salts used to melt winter snow. As the snow melted into water, passing vehicles would literally spray the piers with salt solution. A number were replaced with aesthetically designed steel "K" bridges, such as this one at Hecla Road. Its predecessor may be seen in the distance in the image on page 61. Unfortunately, the K bridges provided no allowance for future widening. (Neal A. Schorr.)

The next issue that needed to be addressed was the under-engineered pavement. Close examination of the above image, taken in the Path Valley on March 22, 1994, reveals "reflection cracking" of the asphalt overlay pavement. This is a process whereby the joints and cracks in the underlying concrete gradually propagate up though the asphalt overlay. Further along in the process, the overlay begins to fail on top of the joints, which then need to be patched. This resulted in an annoying rhythmic thumping as one drove down the road. The only way to permanently solve the problem was to tear out pavement, then build an adequately engineered roadway including a crushed stone base. Beginning in 1999, this was exactly what was done to this same stretch of highway. The image below is a contemporary photograph of the same general area. Gone is the bumpy pavement that plagued the turnpike for so many years. Surprisingly, the commission elected to retain the highway's original geometry, including the narrow 10-foot median. As a result, even after reconstruction, it still looked like the same old highway. (Above, Mitchell E. Dakelman; below, Neal A. Schorr.)

With time, more and more areas of the turnpike required reconstruction as the original pavement neared the end of its useful service life. This is an image of the highway a few miles west of Allegheny Mountain Tunnel. Unlike the section in the Path Valley, here the median was widened to 24 feet. Now the inside shoulder was wide enough to accommodate a disabled vehicle, and the additional distance between the barrier and passing vehicles made the road much easier to drive. This segment had a number of overpasses that also required replacement. Unfortunately, they were replaced with strictly utilitarian structures with no allowance for future widening of the highway. (Neal A. Schorr.)

Finally, in the early 2000s, the Pennsylvania Turnpike Commission adopted a completely new design that would fully bring the Pennsylvania Turnpike up to the design standards of contemporary highways. Gone at last was the narrow median, now replaced with a 26-foot-wide median, including 12-foot-wide left-hand shoulders that could accommodate a disabled vehicle of any size. Furthermore, all newly reconstructed areas were built with six rather than four lanes. This accommodated the never-ending increase in traffic volume. More importantly, with an extra lane available, trucks were now prohibited from the left lane. This eliminated the unnerving sensation of being boxed in by tractor trailers moving at high speed while the driver was plastered up against the median barrier to the left. (Christine Baker, Pennsylvania Turnpike Commission.)

While the original highway respected aesthetics with its use of decorative masonry work on the rigid-frame concrete-arch bridges, this practice had largely fallen by the wayside as bridges were replaced by new ones of strictly functional design. With the adoption of the new six-lane cross-section, a new bridge design was chosen that could incorporate attractive architectural details. Many were constructed with simulated stone or brick wing walls and parapets, such as this one at the Blue Mountain interchange. (Neal A. Schorr.)

In a few instances, original structures were restored to their 1940 appearance. A case in point is this rigid-frame concrete overpass at the Willow Hill interchange. This section of the highway was rebuilt and slightly widened, which required replacement of the southern side of the structure. Rather than simply reconstructing it as a featureless concrete wall, the turnpike commission accurately reproduced the architectural details of the original bridge. While several factors did not permit the same to be done with the parapet, the result is a rehabilitated structure that recalls the turnpike as it appeared the day it opened. The above image shows the overall appearance of the rehabilitated structure, while the photograph at right reveals how the structure was widened. (Both, Neal A. Schorr.)

The commission's efforts in recalling the turnpike's glory years extended to the service plaza structures as well. As with the roadway and bridges, the buildings had reached the end of their useful lives and needed to be replaced. Rather than just replacing them with contemporary structures, the commission wisely directed that their replacements be of the same architectural style as the originals. The result was a series of richly detailed structures, once more built of stone that recalled the buildings constructed around 1940. The above image is that of North Midway. But unlike the originals, their interiors were completely modern in design, as seen in the photograph below taken at South Somerset. All featured a variety of quick-serve food vendors surrounding a central food court, as well as a convenience store and a self-serve gasoline station. (Both, Neal A. Schorr.)

The commission went a step further with the reconstruction of South Midway. Although the interior of the original building would be demolished, the stone exterior was preserved. New entrances were provided on either end, and their general architectural style was the same as that of the original structure. In between, the restored exterior appeared almost identical to the original structure, including the retention of the frame dining room extension at the western end of the building. (Neal A. Schorr.)

While most of the interior was demolished, a new facility was created that recalled the elegant interior of the plaza's Howard Johnson's restaurant. Though food service was now provided by a variety of vendors, the food court was designed to resemble the original dining room. Both of the structure's large fireplaces were preserved and were incorporated into the new dining facility. The above photograph shows the fireplace at the eastern end of the structure, as well as the wooden trim reminiscent of the original interior. Framed photographs depicting the early years of the turnpike hang from the walls. The image below shows the entrance lobby at the western end of the building. For the first time, the Pennsylvania Turnpike has created a public display that commemorates the highway's rich history. The display includes souvenirs once sold at the service plaza gift shops, turnpike postcards, and publications dealing with the turnpike, including the July 29, 1940, issue of *Life* magazine featuring Herbert Gehr's photo essay "Super-highway." The display enables today's travelers, most of whom were born long after the glory years of the Pennsylvania Turnpike, to understand why for many years it really was "The World's Greatest Highway." (Both, Neal A. Schorr.)

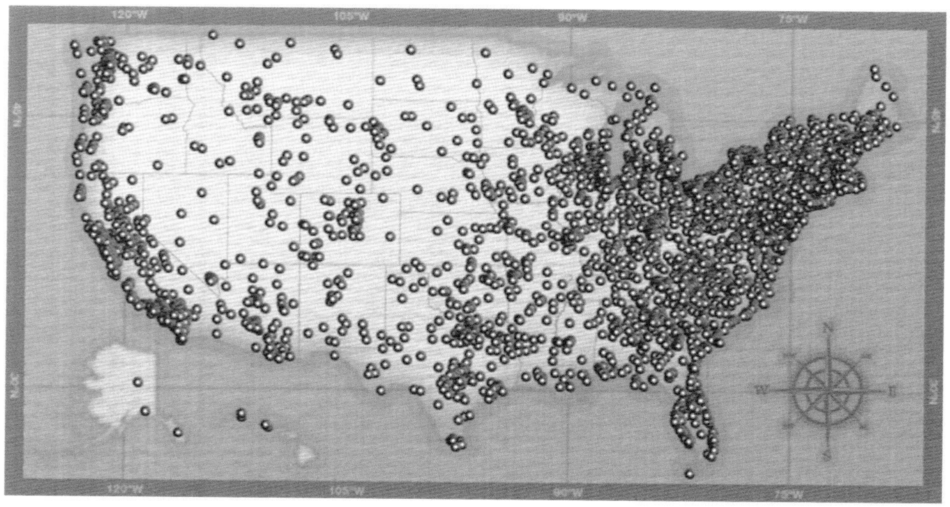